Cannibal Capitalism

Cannibal Capitalism

How Our System Is Devouring Democracy, Care, and the Planet—and What We Can Do about It

Nancy Fraser

VERSO
London • New York

This paperback edition first published by Verso 2023
First published by Verso 2022

1 3 5 7 9 10 8 6 4 2

Verso
UK: 6 Meard Street, London W1F 0EG
US: 388 Atlantic Avenue, Brooklyn, NY 11217
versobooks.com

Verso is the imprint of New Left Books

ISBN-13: 978-1-80429-258-7 (PB)
ISBN-13: 978-1-83976-125-6 (US EBK)
ISBN-13: 978-1-83976-124-9 (UK EBK)

British Library Cataloguing in Publication Data
A catalogue record for this book is available from the British Library

Library of Congress Cataloging-in-Publication Data
A catalog record for this book is available from the Library of Congress

Typeset in Sabon by MJ & N Gavan, Truro, Cornwall
Printed and bound by CPI Group (UK) Ltd, Croydon CR0 4YY

for Robin Blackburn and Rahel Jaeggi,
indispensable dialogue partners and dear friends

Contents

Acknowledgments

It is common to think of a book as the fruit of its author's individual labor. But that view is deeply misleading. Virtually every writer relies on a host of enabling background conditions —financial support and library access, editorial guidance and research assistance, collegial criticism and inspiration, encouragement from friends, and care from intimates and family members. These constitute the "hidden abodes" of authorship, to invoke a phrase that plays a key role in the pages that follow. Too often relegated to the backstage, while the author preens in front, they are indispensable conditions for a book's publication. Without them it could not see the light of day.

Clearly, a book that theorizes the hidden supports of capitalist production must acknowledge its own underpinnings. These came in many forms and from many sources. On the institutional front, the New School for Social Research provided a flexible teaching arrangement, a year of sabbatical leave, and (most important of all) an environment of intellectual vibrancy. Dartmouth College hosted me as Roth Family Distinguished Visiting Scholar in 2017–18 and later gave me a second academic home with a superb library, generous funding, and accomplished colleagues.

Several other institutions gave me precious time and collegial surroundings in which to develop the ideas in this book. Warmest thanks to Jude Browne and the University of Cambridge Centre for Gender Studies; to Michel Wieviorka and the Collège d'études mondiales; to Rainer Forst and the Justitia

Amplificata Centre for Advanced Studies, Frankfurt, and the Forschungskolleg Humanwissenschaften, Bad Homburg; to Hartmut Rosa and the Research Group on Post-Growth Societies, Friedrich-Schiller-Universität, Jena; and to Winfried Fluck, Ulla Haselstein, the Einstein Foundation of Berlin, and the JFK Institute for American Studies, Frei Universität, Berlin.

I relied throughout on the research skills and camaraderie of an extraordinary group of graduate assistants. My heartfelt gratitude goes to Blair Taylor, Brian Milstein, Mine Yildirim, Mayra Cotta, Daniel Boscov-Ellen, Tatiana Llaguno Nieves, Anastasiia Kalk, and Rosa Martins.

Several journals, but especially *New Left Review* and *Critical Historical Studies*, gave me the precious opportunity to circulate early accounts of the ideas expounded here and to receive feedback that helped me refine them. The specifics of my debts to them and to others who published previous formulations of these ideas are acknowledged below.

Verso provided the editor I've always dreamed of in Jessie Kindig, whose enthusiasm, creativity, and way with words made all the difference. Also at Verso, production editor Daniel O'Connor and copyeditor Stan Smith transformed a messy and much revised manuscript into a finished, error-free set of pages. Under the direction of Melissa Weiss, David Gee designed a standout cover, at once elegant and (dare I say) biting.

Behind this book, too, stands the indispensable support of colleagues and friends. I have thanked some of them in the notes to individual chapters, where their influence loomed especially large. But some have shaped and inspired my thoughts more broadly and over the longer haul. Among these steadfast companions and dialogue partners, I thank Cinzia Arruzza, Banu Bargu, Seyla Benhabib, Richard J. Bernstein, Luc Boltanski, Craig Calhoun, Michael Dawson, Duncan Foley, Rainer Forst, Jürgen Habermas, David Harvey, Axel Honneth, Johanna Oksala, Andreas Malm, Jane Mansbridge, Chantal Mouffe, Donald Pease, the late Moishe Postone,

Hartmut Rosa, Antonia Soulez, Wolfgang Streeck, Cornel West, and Michel Wieviorka.

Two more, to whom this book is dedicated, were in my thoughts and heart throughout the writing. I thank Robin Blackburn, on whose erudition, insight, and kindness I relied again and again; and Rahel Jaeggi, my true partner in "conversation," with whom many of the ideas presented here were originally developed and later improved.

Lastly, there is Eli Zaretsky, whose support for this book was so profound, multi-faceted, and pervasive as to defy any summary statement. Let's just say that *Cannibal Capitalism* wouldn't exist without his probing intelligence, largeness of vision, and sustaining love.

Earlier versions of several of these chapters have been previously published and appear here in revised form, with permission from their original publishers.

An earlier version of chapter 1 was delivered as the 2014 Diane Middlebrook and Carl Djerassi Lecture at the University of Cambridge on February 7, 2014, and later published in *New Left Review*, issue 86 (2014), as "Behind Marx's Hidden Abode: For an Expanded Conception of Capitalism." Its arguments went through a baptism of fire, and came out the stronger for it, through challenging discussions with Rahel Jaeggi, many of which are recorded in our coauthored book *Capitalism: A Conversation in Critical Theory*, edited by Brian Milstein (to be republished by Verso in April 2023). Thanks again to Jaeggi for her probing intelligence and warmhearted friendship.

An earlier version of chapter 2 was first delivered as the presidential address at the one hundred fourteenth Eastern Division meeting of the American Philosophical Association in Savannah, Georgia, on January 5, 2018, and later published in *Proceedings and Addresses of the American Philosophical Association*, volume 92 (2018), as "Is Capitalism *Necessarily*

Racist?" I am grateful to Robin Blackburn, Sharad Chari, Rahel Jaeggi, and Eli Zaretsky for helpful comments on this chapter, to Daniel Boscov-Ellen for research assistance, and especially to Michael Dawson for inspiration and stimulation.

An earlier version of chapter 3 was first delivered as the thirty-eighth annual Marc Bloch Lecture at the École des hautes études en sciences sociales in Paris on June 14, 2016, and later published in *New Left Review*, issue 100 (2016), as "Contradictions of Capitalism and Care." Many of its arguments were developed in conversation with Cinzia Arruzza and Johanna Oksala, to whom I am deeply grateful.

Earlier versions of chapter 4 were delivered in Vienna as the inaugural lecture of the first Karl Polanyi Visiting Professorship on May 4, 2021, as "Incinerating Nature: Why Global Warming is Baked into Capitalist Society," and published in *New Left Review*, issue 127 (2021), as "Climates of Capital: For a Trans-environmental Eco-socialism."

Earlier versions of chapter 5 were published, first, in *Critical Historical Studies*, volume 2 (2015), as "Legitimation Crisis? On the Political Contradictions of Financialized Capitalism," and later in German translation in *Was stimmt nicht mit der Demokratie? Eine Debatte mit Klaus Dörre, Nancy Fraser, Stephan Lessenich und Hartmut Rosa*, edited by Hanna Ketterer and Karina Becker (Suhrkamp Verlag, 2019).

An earlier version of chapter 6 was first delivered as the 2019 Solomon Katz Distinguished Lecture in the Humanities at the University of Washington, May 8, 2019, and later published in *Socialist Register*, volume 56, *Beyond Market Dystopia: New Ways of Living* (2019), as "What Should Socialism Mean in the 21st Century?"

Preface

Cannibal Capitalism: Are We Toast?

Readers of this book don't need me to tell them that we're in trouble. They're already tuned in to, indeed reeling from, a tangle of looming threats and realized miseries: crushing debt, precarious work, and besieged livelihoods; dwindling services, crumbling infrastructures, and hardened borders; racialized violence, deadly pandemics, and extreme weather—all overarched by political dysfunctions that block our ability to envision and implement solutions. None of this is breaking news, and none needs belaboring here.

What this book *does* offer is a deep dive into the source of all these horribles. It diagnoses what drives the malady and names the perp. "Cannibal capitalism" is my term for the social system that has brought us to this point. To see why the term is apt, let's consider each of the *c*-words that make it up.

"Cannibalism" has several meanings. The most familiar, and the most concrete, is the ritual eating of human flesh by a human being. Burdened by a long racist history, the term was applied by an inverted logic to Black Africans on the receiving end of Euro-imperial predation. So there's a certain satisfaction in turning the tables and invoking it here as a descriptor for the capitalist class—a group, this book will show, that feeds off everyone else. But the term also has a more abstract meaning, which captures a deeper truth about our society. The verb "to cannibalize" means to deprive one facility or enterprise of an essential element of its functioning for the purpose of creating or sustaining another one. That, we'll see, is a fair approximation of the relation of capitalism's economy to the system's non-economic precincts: to the families and communities, habitats and ecosystems, state capacities and public powers whose substance its economy consumes to engorge itself.

There is also a specialized astronomical meaning: a celestial object is said to cannibalize another such object when it incorporates mass from the latter through gravitational attraction. That, I will show here, too, is an apt characterization of the process by which capital draws into its orbit natural and social wealth from peripheral zones of the world system. There is, finally, the ouroboros, the self-cannibalizing serpent that eats its own tail, depicted on this book's cover. That's a fitting image, we'll also see, for a system that's wired to devour the social, political, and natural bases of its own existence —which are also the bases of ours. All told, the cannibal metaphor offers several promising avenues for an analysis of capitalist society. It invites us to see that society as an institutionalized feeding frenzy—in which the main course is us.

"Capitalism," too, cries out for clarification. The word is commonly used to name an economic system based on private property and market exchange, wage labor and production for profit. But that definition is too narrow, obscuring rather than disclosing the system's true nature. "Capitalism," I'll argue here, better designates something larger: a societal order that empowers a profit-driven economy to prey on the extra-economic supports it needs to function—wealth expropriated from nature and subject peoples; multiple forms of carework, chronically undervalued when not wholly disavowed; public goods and public powers, which capital both requires and tries to curtail; the energy and creativity of working people. Although they do not appear on corporate balance sheets, these forms of wealth are essential preconditions for the profits and gains that do. Vital underpinnings of accumulation, they, too, are constitutive components of the capitalist order.

In this book, accordingly, "capitalism" refers not to a type of economy but to a type of *society*: one that authorizes an officially designated economy to pile up monetized value for investors and owners, while devouring the non-economized wealth of everyone else. Serving that wealth on a platter to the corporate classes, this society invites them to make a meal of our creative capacities and of the earth that sustains us—with no obligation to replenish what they consume or repair what they damage. And that is a recipe for trouble. Like the ouroboros that eats its own tail, capitalist society is primed to devour its own substance. A veritable dynamo of self-destabilization, it periodically precipitates crises while routinely eating away at the bases of our existence.

Cannibal capitalism, then, is the system to which we owe the present crisis. Truth be told, it's a rare type of crisis, in which multiple bouts of gluttony have converged. What we face, thanks to decades of financialization, is not "only" a crisis of rampaging inequality and low-waged precarious work; nor "merely" one of care or social reproduction; nor "just" a crisis of migration and racialized violence. Neither is it "simply" an ecological crisis in which a heating planet disgorges lethal plagues, nor "only" a political crisis featuring hollowed-out infrastructure, ramped-up militarism, and a proliferation of strongmen. Oh no, it's something worse: a general crisis of the entire societal order in which all those calamities converge, exacerbating one another and threatening to swallow us whole.

This book maps that massive tangle of dysfunction and domination. Expanding our view of capitalism to include the extra-economic ingredients of capital's diet, it brings together in a single frame *all* the oppressions, contradictions, and conflicts of the present conjuncture. In this frame, structural injustice means class exploitation, to be sure, but also gender domination and racial/imperial oppression—both non-accidental by-products of a societal order that subordinates social reproduction to commodity production and that demands racialized expropriation to underwrite profitable exploitation. As understood here, likewise, the system's contradictions incline it not only to economic crises but also to crises of care, ecology, and politics, all of which are in full flower today, courtesy of the long spell of corporate bingeing known as neoliberalism.

As I conceive it, lastly, cannibal capitalism precipitates a broad array and complex mix of social struggles: not just class struggles at the point of production, but also boundary struggles at the system's constitutive joints. Where production butts up against social reproduction, the system incites conflicts over care, both public and private, paid and unpaid. Where exploitation crosses expropriation, it foments struggles over "race," migration, and empire. Then too, where accumulation hits natural bedrock, cannibal capitalism sparks conflicts over land and energy, flora and fauna, the fate of the earth. Finally, where global markets and megacorporations meet national states and institutions of transnational governance, it provokes struggles over the shape, control, and reach of public power. All these strands of our present predicament find their place in an expanded conception of capitalism that is simultaneously unitary and differentiated.

Armed with this conception, *Cannibal Capitalism* poses a pressing existential question: "Are we toast?" Can we figure out how to dismantle the social system that is driving us into the jaws of obliteration? Can we come together to address the entire crisis complex that system has spawned—not "just" the heating of the earth, nor "only" the progressive destruction of our collective capacities for public action, nor "merely" the wholesale assault on our ability to care for one another and sustain social ties, nor "simply" the disproportionate dumping of the ensuing fallout on poor, working-class, and racialized populations, but the *general* crisis in which these various harms are intertwined? Can we envision an emancipatory, counterhegemonic project of eco-societal transformation of sufficient breadth and vision to coordinate the struggles of multiple social movements, political parties, labor unions, and other collective actors—a project aimed at laying the cannibal to rest once and for all? In the current conjuncture, I argue here, nothing short of such a project can avail.

Once we expand our view of capitalism, moreover, we must also expand our vision of what should replace it. Whether we call it socialism or something else, the alternative we seek cannot aim to reorganize the system's economy alone. It must also reorganize the latter's relation to all those forms of wealth it currently cannibalizes. What must be reinvented, then, is the relation of production to reproduction, of private to public power, of human society to nonhuman nature. If this sounds like a tall order, it's our best hope. Only by thinking big can we give ourselves a fighting chance to vanquish cannibal capitalism's relentless drive to eat us whole.

1

Omnivore: Why We Need to Expand Our Conception of Capitalism

Capitalism is back! After decades in which the term could scarcely be found outside the writings of Marxist thinkers, commentators of varying stripes now worry openly about its sustainability, scholars from every school scramble to systematize criticisms of it, and activists throughout the world mobilize in opposition to its practices. Certainly, the return of "capitalism" is a welcome development, a crystal-clear marker, if any were needed, of the depth of the present crisis—and of the pervasive hunger for a systematic account of it. What all the talk about capitalism indicates, symptomatically, is a growing awareness that the heterogeneous ills—financial, economic, ecological, political, social—that surround us can be traced to a common root; and that reforms that fail to engage with the deep structural underpinnings of these ills are doomed to fail. Equally, the term's renaissance signals the wish in many quarters for an analysis that clarifies the relations among the disparate social struggles of our time—an analysis that could foster the close cooperation, if not the full unification, of their most advanced, progressive currents within a counter-systemic bloc. The hunch that such an analysis should center on capitalism is on the mark.

Nevertheless, the current boom in capitalism talk remains largely rhetorical—more a symptom of the desire for systematic critique than a substantive contribution to it. Thanks to decades of social amnesia, whole generations of younger activists and scholars have become sophisticated practitioners of discourse analysis while remaining utterly innocent of the traditions of *Kapitalkritik*. They are only now beginning to ask how the latter could be practiced today to clarify the current conjuncture.

Their "elders," veterans of previous eras of anti-capitalist ferment who might have provided some guidance, are burdened with blinders of their own. They have largely failed, despite professed good intentions, to incorporate the insights of feminist, ecological, postcolonial, and Black liberation thought into their understandings of capitalism in a systematic way.

The upshot is that we are living through a capitalist crisis of great severity without a critical theory that clarifies it—let alone points us toward an emancipatory resolution. Certainly, today's crisis does not fit the standard models that we have inherited: it is multidimensional, encompassing not only the official economy, including finance, but also such "noneconomic" phenomena as global warming, "care deficits," and the hollowing out of public power at every scale. Yet our received models of crisis tend to focus exclusively on the economic aspects, which they isolate from, and privilege over, other facets. Equally important, today's crisis is generating novel political configurations and grammars of social conflict. Struggles over nature, social reproduction, dispossession, and public power are central to this constellation, implicating multiple axes of inequality, including nationality/race-ethnicity, religion, sexuality, and class. In this respect, too, however, our received theoretical models fail us, as they continue to prioritize struggles over labor at the point of production. In general, then, we lack conceptions of capitalism and capitalist crisis that are adequate to our time.

Cannibal capitalism, I contend, is such a conception. I introduce it in this chapter by asking what lies behind Karl Marx's principal argument in *Capital*, Volume I. That work has much to offer in the way of general conceptual resources; and it is in principle open to the broader concerns I just mentioned. Yet it fails to reckon systematically with gender, race, ecology, and political power as structuring axes of inequality in capitalist societies—let alone as stakes and premises of social struggle. Thus its best insights need to be reconstructed. Here, accordingly, my strategy is to look first *at* Marx, and then *behind* him, in the hope of shedding new light on some old questions: What exactly *is* capitalism? And how is it best conceptualized? Should we think of it as an economic system, a form of ethical life, or an institutionalized societal order? How should we characterize its "crisis tendencies," and where should we locate them?

Defining Features of Capitalism, According to Marx

I begin by recalling what Marx took to be capitalism's defining features. Thus, the train of thought I shall follow to cannibal capitalism will appear at first sight to be orthodox. But I intend to de-orthodoxize it shortly, by showing how these features presuppose some others, which constitute their background conditions of possibility. Just as Marx looked behind the sphere of exchange, into the "hidden abode" of production, in order to discover capitalism's secrets, I shall seek production's conditions of possibility behind that sphere, in realms that are more hidden still.

For Marx, the first defining feature of capitalism is private property in the means of production, which presupposes a class division between the owners and the producers. This division arose as a result of the breakup of a previous social world in which most people, however differently situated, had access to the means of subsistence and means of production; access, in other words, to food, shelter, and clothing, and to tools, land, and work, without having to go through a labor market. Capitalism decisively overturned such arrangements. It enclosed the commons, abrogated the customary use rights of the majority, and transformed shared resources into the private property of a small minority.

That leads directly to Marx's second core feature: the free labor market. Once separated from the means of production, the vast majority had to go through that peculiar institution in order to work and get what they needed to continue living and to raise their children. It is worth stressing just how bizarre, how "unnatural," how historically anomalous and specific the free labor market is. Labor is "free" here in a double sense: first, in terms of legal status—not enslaved, enserfed, entailed, or otherwise bound to a given place or particular master—and hence mobile and able to enter into a labor contract. But second, it is "free" from access to means of subsistence and means of production, including from customary use rights in land and tools—and hence bereft of the resources and entitlements that could permit one to abstain from the labor market. Thus, capitalism is defined in part by its constitution and use of (doubly) free wage labor—even though, as we shall see, it also relies on a great deal of labor that is unfree or dependent, unacknowledged or unremunerated.

Next is the equally strange phenomenon of "self"-expanding value, which is Marx's third core feature.[1] Capitalism is peculiar in having an objective systemic thrust: namely, the accumulation of capital. Accordingly, everything the owners do *qua* capitalists is aimed at the expansion of their capital. Like the producers, they too stand under a peculiar systemic compulsion. Everyone's efforts to satisfy their needs are indirect, harnessed to something else that assumes priority—an overriding imperative inscribed in an impersonal system, capital's own drive to unending "self"-expansion. Marx is brilliant on this point. In a capitalist society, he says, capital itself becomes the Subject. Human beings are its pawns, reduced to figuring out how they can get what they need in the interstices while feeding the beast.

The fourth feature specifies the distinctive role of markets in capitalist society. Markets have existed throughout human history, including in noncapitalist societies. Their functioning under capitalism, however, is distinguished by two further characteristics. First, markets serve in capitalist society to allocate the major inputs to commodity production. Understood by bourgeois political economy as "factors of production," these inputs were originally identified as land, labor, and capital. In addition to utilizing markets to allocate labor, capitalism also uses them to allocate real estate, capital goods, raw materials, and credit. Insofar as it allocates these productive inputs through market mechanisms, capitalism transforms them into commodities. It is, in the Cambridge economist Piero Sraffa's arresting phrase, a system for the "production of commodities by means of commodities," albeit one that also relies, as we shall see, on a background of non-commodities.[2]

But there is also a second key function that markets assume in a capitalist society: they determine how society's surplus will be invested. By "surplus," Marx meant the collective fund of social energies exceeding those required to reproduce a given form of life and to replenish what is used up in the course of living it. How a society uses its surplus capacities is absolutely central, raising fundamental questions about how people want to live—where they choose to invest their collective energies, how they propose to balance "productive work" vis-à-vis family life, leisure, and other activities—as well as how they aspire to relate to nonhuman nature and what they aim to leave to future generations. Capitalist societies tend to leave such decisions to "market forces." This is perhaps their most consequential and perverse characteristic, the handing over of the most important matters to a mechanism geared to the quantitative expansion of monetized value and congenitally oblivious to qualitative metrics of social wealth and human well-being. It is closely related to our third core feature: capital's inherent but blind directionality, the "self"-expansionary process through which it constitutes itself as the subject of history, displacing the human beings who have made it and turning them into its servants.

By stressing these two roles of markets, I aim to counter the widely held view that capitalism propels the ever-increasing commodification of life as such. That view leads down a blind alley, I think, to dystopian fantasies of a totally commodified world. Not only do such fantasies neglect the emancipatory aspects of markets, but they overlook the fact, stressed by the world-systems theorist Immanuel Wallerstein, that capitalism has often operated on the basis of "semi-proletarianized" households. Under these arrangements, which allow owners to pay workers less, many households derive a portion of their sustenance from sources other than cash wages, including self-provisioning (the garden plot, sewing), informal reciprocity (mutual aid, in-kind transactions), and state transfers (welfare benefits, social services, public goods).[3] Such arrangements leave a sizeable portion of activities and goods outside the purview of the market. They are not mere residual holdovers from precapitalist times; nor are they on their way out. So, for example, mid-twentieth-century Fordism was able to promote working-class consumerism in the industrialized countries of the core only by way of semi-proletarianized households that combined male employment with female homemaking, as well as by inhibiting the development of commodity consumption in the periphery. Semi-proletarianization is even more pronounced in neoliberalism, which has built an entire accumulation strategy by expelling billions of people from the official economy into informal grey zones, from which capital siphons off wealth. As we shall see, this sort of "primitive accumulation" is an ongoing process from which capital profits and on which it relies.

The point, then, is that marketized aspects of capitalist societies coexist with non-marketized aspects. This is no fluke or empirical contingency, but a feature built into capitalism's

DNA. In fact, "coexistence" is too weak a term to capture the relation between marketized and non-marketized aspects of a capitalist society. Better terms would be "functional imbrication" or "dependence," but these fail to convey the perversity of this relation."[4] That aspect, which will become clear soon, is best expressed by "cannibalization."

Behind Marx's "Hidden Abode"

So far, I have elaborated a fairly orthodox definition of capitalism, based on four core features that seem to be "economic." I have effectively followed Marx in looking behind the commonsense perspective, which focuses on market exchange, to the "hidden abode" of production. Now, however, I want to look behind that hidden abode, to see what is more hidden still. My claim is that Marx's account of capitalist production only makes sense when we start to fill in its background conditions of possibility. So the next question will be: What must exist behind these core features in order for them to be possible?

Marx himself broaches a question of this sort near the end of Volume I of *Capital* in the chapter on so-called "primitive" or original accumulation.[5] Where did capital come from? he asks. How did private property in the means of production come to exist, and how did the producers become separated from them? In the preceding chapters, Marx had laid bare capitalism's economic logic in abstraction from its background conditions of possibility, which were assumed as simply given. But it turned out that there was a whole backstory about where capital itself comes from—a rather violent story of dispossession and expropriation. Moreover, as theorists from Rosa Luxemburg to David Harvey have stressed, this backstory is not located only in the past, at the "origins" of capitalism.[6] Expropriation is an ongoing, albeit unofficial, mechanism of accumulation, which continues alongside the official mechanism of exploitation—Marx's "front story," so to speak.

This move, from the front story of exploitation to the backstory of expropriation, constitutes a major epistemic shift, which casts everything that went before in a different light. It is analogous to the move Marx makes earlier, near the beginning of Volume I, when he invites us to leave behind the sphere of market exchange, and the perspective of bourgeois common sense associated with it, for the hidden abode of production, which affords a more critical perspective. As a result of that first move, we discover a dirty secret: accumulation proceeds via exploitation. Capital expands, in other words, not via the exchange of equivalents, as the market perspective suggests, but precisely through its opposite: via the non-compensation of a portion of workers' labor time. Similarly, when we move, at the volume's end, from exploitation to expropriation, we discover an even dirtier secret: behind the sublimated coercion of wage labor lie overt violence and outright theft. In other words, the long elaboration of capitalism's economic logic, which constitutes most of Volume I, is not the last word. It is followed by a move to another perspective, the dispossession perspective. This move to what lies behind the "hidden abode" is also a move to history—and to what I have been calling the background conditions of possibility for exploitation.

Arguably, however, Marx did not unfold the full implications of this epistemic shift from exploitation to the still more hidden abode of expropriation. Nor did he theorize some other equally momentous epistemic shifts that are implied in his account of capitalism. These moves, to abodes that are even more hidden, are still in need of conceptualization, as are the full implications of "primitive" accumulation. All of these matters need to be written up in new volumes of *Capital*, if you like, if we are to develop an adequate understanding of twenty-first-century capitalism.

From Commodity Production to Social Reproduction

One essential epistemic shift is that from production to social reproduction—the forms of provisioning, caregiving, and interaction that produce and sustain human beings and social bonds. Variously called "care," "affective labor," or "subjectivation," this activity forms capitalism's human subjects, sustaining them as embodied natural beings, while also constituting them as social beings, forming their *habitus* and the socio-ethical substance, or *Sittlichkeit*, in which they move. Central here is the work of birthing and socializing the young, building communities, producing and reproducing the shared meanings, affective dispositions, and horizons of value that underpin social cooperation. In capitalist societies much, though not all, of this activity goes on outside the market, in households, neighborhoods, and a host of public institutions, including schools and childcare centers; and much of it, though not all, does not take the form of wage labor. Yet social-reproductive activity is absolutely necessary to the existence of waged work, the accumulation of surplus value, and the functioning of capitalism as such. Wage labor could not exist in the absence of housework, child-rearing, schooling, affective care, and a host of other activities which help to produce new generations of workers and replenish existing ones, as well as to maintain social bonds and shared understandings. Much like "original accumulation," therefore, social reproduction is an indispensable background condition of commodity production.

Structurally, moreover, the division between social reproduction and commodity production is central to capitalism —indeed, it is an artifact of it. As scores of feminist theorists have stressed, the distinction is deeply gendered, with reproduction associated with women and production with men. Historically, the split between "productive" waged work and unwaged "reproductive" labor has underpinned modern capitalist forms of women's subordination. Like that between owners and workers, this division too rests on the breakup of a previous world. In this case, what was shattered was a world in which women's work, although distinguished from men's, was nevertheless visible and publicly acknowledged, an integral part of the social universe. With capitalism, by contrast, reproductive labor is split off, relegated to a separate, "private" domestic sphere where its social importance is obscured. And in this new world, where money is a primary medium of power, the fact of its being unpaid or underpaid seals the matter: those who do this work are structurally subordinate to those who earn cash wages in "production," even as their "reproductive" work also supplies necessary preconditions for wage labor.

Far from being universal, then, the division between production and reproduction arose historically, with capitalism. But it was not simply given once and for all. On the contrary, the division mutated over time, taking different forms in different phases of capitalist development. During the twentieth century, some aspects of social reproduction were transformed into public services and public goods, de-privatized but not commodified. Today, the division is shifting again, as neoliberalism privatizes and commodifies these services anew, while also commodifying other aspects of social reproduction for the first time. Moreover, by demanding the retrenchment of public provision while at the same time heavily recruiting women into low-waged service work, this current form of capitalism is remapping the institutional boundaries that previously separated commodity production from social reproduction—and reconfiguring the gender order in the process. Equally important, it is cannibalizing social reproduction, allowing capital to devour the latter freely and without replenishment. The effect, as we shall see in chapter 3, is to turn this vital condition for accumulation into a major flashpoint of capitalist crisis.

From Economy to Ecology

We should also consider a second, equally momentous shift in epistemic perspective, which directs us to another hidden abode. This one is best embodied in the work of ecosocialist thinkers who are now writing another backstory, focused on capitalism's cannibalization of nature. This story concerns capital's annexation—what Rosa Luxemburg called its *Landnahme*—of nature, both as a source of "inputs" to production and as a "sink" to absorb the latter's waste. Nature here is made into a resource for capital, one whose value is both presupposed and disavowed. Treated as costless in capital's accounts, it is freely or cheaply appropriated without repair or replenishment, on the tacit assumption that nature is capable of infinite self-restoration. Thus, the earth's capacity to support life and renew itself constitutes another necessary background condition for commodity production and capital accumulation—and another object of cannibalization.

Structurally capitalism assumes, indeed inaugurates, a sharp division between a natural realm—conceived as offering a free and constant supply of "raw material" available for appropriation—and an economic realm, conceived as a sphere of value, produced by and for human beings. Along with this goes the hardening of a preexisting distinction between Humanity—seen as spiritual, sociocultural, and historical—and (nonhuman) Nature, seen as material, objectively given, and ahistorical. The sharpening of this distinction, too, rests on the breakup of a previous world, in which the rhythms of social life were in many respects adapted to those of nonhuman nature. Capitalism brutally separated human beings from natural, seasonal rhythms, conscripting them into industrial manufacturing, powered by fossil fuels, and profit-driven agriculture, bulked up by chemical fertilizers. Introducing what Marx called a "metabolic rift," it inaugurated what has been misleadingly dubbed the Anthropocene, an entirely new geological era in which "human activity" (really, capital) is cannibalizing the planet.[7]

Arising with capitalism, this division, too, has mutated in the course of the system's development. The current neoliberal phase has inaugurated a new round of enclosures—the commodification of water, for example—which are bringing "more of nature" (if one can speak that way) into the economic front story. At the same time, neoliberalism promises to blur the nature/human boundary: witness new reproductive technologies and the ongoing evolution of cyborgs.[8] Far from offering a "reconciliation" with nature, however, these developments intensify capital's cannibalization of it. Unlike the land enclosures Marx wrote about, which "merely" marketized already-existing natural phenomena, the new enclosures penetrate deep "inside" nature, altering its internal grammar. Finally, neoliberalism is marketizing environmentalism: consider the brisk trade in carbon permits and offsets and in "environmental derivatives," which draw capital away from the long-term, large-scale investment needed to transform unsustainable forms of life premised on fossil fuels. As we shall see in chapter 4, this assault on what remains of the ecological commons is turning the natural condition of capital accumulation into another central node of capitalist crisis.

From the Economic to the Political

Next, let us consider a third major epistemic shift, which points to capitalism's political conditions of possibility: its reliance on public powers to establish and enforce its constitutive norms. Capitalism is inconceivable, after all, in the absence of a legal framework underpinning private enterprise and market exchange. Its front story depends crucially on public powers to guarantee property rights, enforce contracts, adjudicate disputes, quell anti-capitalist rebellions, and maintain the money supply that constitutes capital's lifeblood. Historically, the public powers in question have mostly been lodged in territorial states, including those that operated transnationally, as colonial or imperial powers. It was the legal systems of such states that established the contours of seemingly depoliticized arenas within which private actors could pursue their "economic" interests, free from overt "political" interference, on the one hand, and from patronage obligations derived from kinship, on the other. Likewise, it was territorial states that mobilized "legitimate force" to put down resistance to the expropriations through which capitalist property relations were originated and sustained. Finally, it was such states that nationalized and underwrote money.[9] Historically, we might say, the state "constituted" the capitalist economy.

Here we encounter another major structural division that is constitutive of capitalist society: that between polity and economy. With this division comes the institutional differentiation of public from private power, of political from economic coercion. Like the other core divisions we have discussed, this one, too, arose as a result of the breakup of a previous world. In this case, what was dismantled was a social world in which economic and political power were effectively fused—as, for example, in feudal society, where control over labor, land, and military force was vested in the single institution of lordship and vassalage. In capitalist society, by contrast, as the political theorist Ellen Meiksins Wood has elegantly shown, economic power and political power are split apart; each is assigned its own sphere, its own medium and modus operandi.[10]

However, capitalism's front story also has political conditions of possibility at the geopolitical level. At issue here is the organization of the broader space in which territorial states are embedded. This is a space in which capital moves quite easily, given its expansionist thrust. But its ability to operate across borders depends on international law, brokered arrangements among the Great Powers, and supranational regimes that partially pacify (in a capital-friendly way) a realm that is often imagined as a state of nature. Throughout its history, capitalism's front story has depended on the military and organizational capacities of a succession of global hegemons, which, as the Braudelian historical sociologist Giovanni Arrighi argued, have sought to foster accumulation on a progressively expanding scale within the framework of a multistate system.[11]

Here we find further structural divisions that are constitutive of capitalist society: the "Westphalian" division between the "domestic" and the "international," on the one hand, and the imperialist division between core and periphery, on the other—both premised on the more fundamental division between an increasingly global capitalist economy organized as a "world system," and a political world organized as an international system of territorial states. We shall see in chapter 5 that these divisions are currently transforming as well, as neoliberalism cannibalizes the political capacities on which capital has historically relied at both the state and geopolitical levels. The effect is to turn "the political" into yet another major site of systemic crisis.

From Exploitation to Expropriation

Finally, we should return to the idea that inspired this whole line of thought: namely, Marx's account of primitive accumulation as a historical precondition for capital accumulation. By reconceiving that idea as an ongoing feature of modern capitalism, rather than as a mark of its immaturity now superseded, we can conceptualize another "abode behind the abode" whose operation is structurally necessary to this social system. The hidden necessity here is expropriation—the forcible seizure, on a continuing basis, of the wealth of subjugated and minoritized peoples. Although it is usually seen as the antithesis of capitalism's signature process of exploitation, expropriation is better conceived as the latter's enabling condition.

To see why, consider that both those "exes" contribute to accumulation, but they do so in different ways. Exploitation transfers value to capital under the guise of a free contractual exchange: in return for the use of their labor power, workers receive wages that (are supposed to) cover their costs of living; while capital appropriates their "surplus labor time," it (supposedly) pays at least for their "necessary labor time." In expropriation, by contrast, capitalists dispense with all such niceties in favor of brute confiscation of others' assets, for which they pay little or nothing; by funneling commandeered labor, land, minerals, and/or energy into their firms' operations, they lower their production costs and raise their profits. Thus, far from excluding one another, expropriation and exploitation work hand in hand. Doubly free wage laborers transform looted "raw materials" on machines powered by confiscated sources of energy. Their wages are kept low by the availability of food grown on stolen lands by indebted peons and of consumer goods produced in sweatshops by unfree or dependent "others," whose own reproduction costs are not fully remunerated. Expropriation thus underlies exploitation and makes it profitable. Far from being confined to the system's beginnings, it is a built-in feature of capitalist society, as constitutive and structurally grounded as exploitation.

Moreover, the distinction between the two exes corresponds to a status hierarchy. On the one hand, exploitable "workers" are accorded the status of rights-bearing individuals and citizens; entitled to state protection, they can freely dispose of their own labor power. On the other hand, expropriable "others" are constituted as unfree, dependent beings; stripped of political protection, they are rendered defenseless and inherently violable. Thus, capitalist society divides the producing classes into two distinct categories of persons: one suitable for "mere" exploitation, the other destined for brute expropriation. That division represents yet another institutionalized fault line of capitalist society—as constitutive and structurally entrenched as those, already discussed, between production and reproduction, society and nature, and polity and economy.

Like those other divisions, moreover, this one undergirds a specific mode of domination in capitalist society: namely racial-cum-imperial oppression. As we shall see in chapter 2, it is overwhelmingly racialized populations who are denied political protection in capitalist society and subjected to repeated violations. We need only mention chattel slaves, colonized subjects, conquered "natives," debt peons, "illegals," convicted felons, racialized subjects of apartheid states and their descendants—all of whom are subject to expropriation not just once (as were those who became citizen-workers) but again and again. Thus, the ex/ex division coincides roughly but unmistakably with the global color line. It entrains a range of structural injustices, including racial oppression, imperialism (old and new), indigenous dispossession, and genocide.

Here, then, is another structural division that is constitutive of capitalist society. Also subject to historical shifts, this division, too, serves as a basis for cannibalization. It is deeply entwined with the others conceptualized here—and with the crises that now beset them. Certainly, the political, ecological, and social-reproductive strands of crisis are inseparable from racialized expropriation in both periphery and core: witness capital's reliance on political powers, both national and transnational, to ensure access and title to stolen lands, coerced labor, and looted minerals; its dependence on racialized zones as dumping grounds for toxic waste and as suppliers of underpaid carework; its resort to status divisions and racial resentments to defuse, displace, or foment political crises. In short, economic, ecological, social, and political crises are inextricably entangled with imperialism and racial oppression—and with the escalating antagonisms associated with them.

Capitalism Is Something Larger than an Economy

Much more could be said on each of these points–and will be said in subsequent chapters. But by now the thrust of my argument should be clear. In filling out my initial account of capitalism, I have shown that its economic foreground features depend on non-economic background conditions. An economic system defined by private property, the accumulation of "self"-expanding value, the market allocation of social surplus and of major inputs to commodity production, including (doubly) free labor, is rendered possible by four crucial background conditions, concerned, respectively, with social reproduction, the earth's ecology, political power, and ongoing infusions of wealth expropriated from racialized peoples. To understand capitalism, therefore, we need to resituate Marx's front story in relation to these four backstories. We must connect the Marxian perspective to other emancipatory currents of critical theorizing: feminist, ecological, political, anti-imperialist, and anti-racist.

What sort of animal is capitalism on this account? The picture I have elaborated here differs importantly from the familiar idea that capitalism is an economic system. Granted, it may have looked at first sight as if the core features we identified were "economic." However, that appearance was misleading. One of the peculiarities of capitalism is that it treats its structuring social relations *as if* they were economic. In fact, we quickly found it necessary to talk about the "non-economic" background conditions that enabled such an "economic system" to exist. These are features not of a capitalist economy, but of a capitalist *society*. Far from airbrushing them out of the picture, we need to integrate them into our understanding of what capitalism is. And that means reconceptualizing capitalism as something larger than an economy.

Likewise, the picture I have sketched differs from the view of capitalism as a reified form of ethical life, characterized by pervasive commodification and monetization. In that view, as articulated in Georg Lukács's celebrated essay on "Reification and the Consciousness of the Proletariat," the commodity form colonizes all of life, stamping its mark on such diverse phenomena as law, science, morality, art, and culture.[12] In my view, by contrast, commodification is far from universal in capitalist society. On the contrary, where it is present, it depends for its very existence on zones of non-commodification, which capital systematically cannibalizes.

Whether social, ecological, or political, none of these non-commodified zones simply mirrors commodity logic. Each embodies distinctive normative and ontological grammars of its own. For example, social practices oriented to reproduction (as opposed to production) tend to engender ideals of care, mutual responsibility, and solidarity.[13] Likewise, practices oriented to polity, as opposed to economy, often refer to principles of democracy, public autonomy, and collective self-determination. Then, too, practices associated with capitalism's background conditions in nonhuman nature tend to foster such values as ecological stewardship, non-domination of nature, and justice between generations. Finally, practices associated with expropriation, or rather with resistance to it, often promote values of integration, on the one hand, and of community autonomy, on the other.

Certainly, these "non-economic" normativities often assume a guise that is hierarchical and parochial (in the case of reproduction), restricted or exclusionary (in the case of polity), romantic and sectarian (in the case of nonhuman nature), and class insensitive and reified (in the case of expropriation). Thus, they should not be idealized. But it is important, nevertheless, to register their divergence from the values associated with capitalism's foreground: above all, growth, efficiency, equal exchange, individual choice, negative liberty, and meritocratic advancement.

This divergence makes all the difference to how we conceptualize capitalism. Far from generating a single, all-pervasive logic of reification, capitalist society is normatively differentiated, encompassing a determinate plurality of distinct but interrelated social ontologies. What happens when these collide remains to be seen. But the structure that underpins them is already clear: capitalism's distinctive normative topography arises from the foreground/background relations we have identified. If we aim to develop a critical theory of it, we must replace the view of capitalism as a reified form of ethical life with a more differentiated, structural view.

If capitalism is neither an economic system nor a reified form of ethical life, then what is it? My answer is that it is best conceived as an institutionalized societal order, on a par with, for example, feudalism. Understanding capitalism in this way underscores its structural divisions, especially the institutional separations that I have identified. Constitutive of capitalism, we have seen, is the institutional separation of "economic production" from "social reproduction," a gendered separation that grounds specifically capitalist forms of male domination, even as it also enables capitalist exploitation of labor power and, through that, its officially sanctioned mode of accumulation. Also definitive of capitalism is the institutional separation of "economy" from "polity"—a separation that expels matters defined as economic from the political agenda of territorial states, freeing capital to roam in a transnational no-man's land where it reaps the benefits of hegemonic ordering while escaping political control. Fundamental to capitalism, too, is the ontological division, preexisting but massively intensified, between its (nonhuman) "natural" background and its (apparently nonnatural) "human" foreground. Equally constitutive, finally, is the exploitation/expropriation division, which twins the (double) freedom of capitalism's official working class with the disavowed subjection of racialized "others." To speak of capitalism as an institutionalized societal order, premised on such separations, is to suggest its non-accidental, structural imbrication with gender domination, ecological degradation, racial/imperial oppression, and political domination—all in conjunction, of course, with its equally structural, non-accidental foreground dynamic of (doubly) free labor exploitation.

Boundary Struggles

This is not to suggest, however, that capitalism's institutional divisions are simply given once and for all. On the contrary, as we have seen, precisely where and how capitalist societies draw the line between production and reproduction, economy and polity, human and nonhuman nature, exploitation and expropriation varies historically, according to the regime of accumulation. In fact, we can conceptualize mercantile capitalism, liberal-colonial capitalism, state-managed monopoly capitalism, and globalizing neoliberal capitalism in precisely these terms: as four historically specific ways of demarcating the various realms that comprise capitalism.

Equally important, the precise configuration of the capitalist order at any place and time depends on contestation—on the balance of social power and on the outcome of political struggles. Far from simply being given, capitalism's institutional divisions often become foci of conflict as actors mobilize to challenge or defend the established boundaries separating economy from polity, production from reproduction, human from nonhuman nature, and exploitation from expropriation. Insofar as they aim to relocate contested processes on the system's institutional map, capitalism's subjects draw on the normative perspectives associated with the various zones that we have identified.

We can see this happening today. For example, some opponents of neoliberalism draw on ideals of care and responsibility, associated with reproduction, in order to oppose efforts to commodify education. Others summon notions of stewardship of nature and justice between generations, associated with ecology, to militate for a shift to renewable energy. Still others invoke ideals of public autonomy, associated with polity, to advocate international capital controls and to extend democratic accountability beyond the state. Yet others cite norms of integration and community autonomy, associated with resistance to expropriation, to advocate prison abolition and police defunding. Such claims, along with the counterclaims they inevitably incite, are the very stuff of social struggle in capitalist societies—as fundamental as the class struggles over control of commodity production and distribution of surplus value that Marx privileged. These *boundary struggles*, as I shall call them, decisively shape the structure of capitalist societies.[14] They play a constitutive role in the view of capitalism as an institutionalized societal order.

The focus on boundary struggles should forestall any misimpression that the view I have been sketching is functionalist —focused, that is, on demonstrating how every instance serves to buttress the system. Granted, I began by characterizing social reproduction, ecology, political power, and expropriation as necessary background conditions for capitalism's economic front story, stressing their functionality for commodity production, labor exploitation, and capital accumulation. But this moment does not capture the full story of capitalism's foreground/background relations. It coexists, rather, with another moment, already hinted at, that is equally central and that emerges from the characterization of social, political, ecological, and peripheralized/expropriable zones as reservoirs of "non-economic" normativity. This implies that, even as these "non-economic" orders make commodity production possible, they are not reducible to that enabling function. Far from being wholly exhausted by, or entirely subservient to, the dynamics of accumulation, each of these hidden abodes harbors distinctive ontologies of social practice and normative ideals.

Moreover, these "non-economic" ideals are pregnant with critical-political possibility. Especially in times of crisis, they can be turned against core economic practices associated with capital accumulation. In such times, the structural divisions that normally serve to segregate the various normativities within their own institutional spheres tend to weaken. When the separations fail to hold, capitalism's subjects—who live, after all, in more than one sphere—experience normative conflict. Far from bringing in ideas from the "outside," they draw on capitalism's own complex normativity to criticize it, mobilizing against the grain the multiplicity of ideals that coexist, at times uneasily, in an institutionalized societal order premised on foreground/background divisions. Thus, the view of capitalism as an institutionalized societal order helps us understand how a critique of capitalism is possible from within it.

Yet this view also suggests that it would be wrong to construe society, polity, nature, and periphery romantically, as "outside" capitalism and as inherently opposed to it. That romantic view is held today by a fair number of anti-capitalist thinkers and left-wing activists, including cultural feminists, deep ecologists, neo-anarchists, and decolonialists, as well as by many proponents of "plural," "post-growth," "subsistence," and "social and solidary" economies. Too often, these currents treat "care," "nature," "direct action," "commoning," or (neo) "communalism" as intrinsically anti-capitalist. As a result, they overlook the fact that their favorite practices are not only sources of critique but also integral parts of the capitalist order.

In my view, by contrast, society, polity, nature, and expropriable periphery arose concurrently with economy and developed in symbiosis with it. They are effectively the latter's "others" and only acquire their specific character in contrast to it. Thus, reproduction and production make a pair, with each term co-defined by way of the other. Neither makes any sense apart from the other. The same is true of polity/economy, nature/human, and core/periphery. Part and parcel of the capitalist order, none of the "non-economic" realms affords a wholly external standpoint that could underwrite an absolutely pure and fully radical form of critique. On the contrary, political projects that appeal to what they imagine to be capitalism's "outside" usually end up recycling capitalist stereotypes, as they counterpose female nurturance to male aggression, spontaneous cooperation to economic calculation, nature's holistic organicism to anthropocentric speciesism, subsistence communalism to occidental individualism. To premise one's struggles on these oppositions is not to challenge but unwittingly to reflect the institutionalized societal order of capitalist society.

It follows from this that a proper account of capitalism's foreground/background relations must hold together three distinct ideas. First, capitalism's "non-economic" realms serve as enabling background conditions for its economy; the latter depends for its very existence on values and inputs from the former. Second, however, capitalism's "non-economic" realms have a weight and character of their own, which can under certain circumstances provide resources for anti-capitalist struggle. Nevertheless—and this is the third point—these realms are part and parcel of capitalist society, historically co-constituted in tandem with its economy, and marked by their symbiosis with it.

Crises of Cannibalization

There is also a fourth idea, which returns us to the problem of crisis with which I began. Capitalism's foreground/background relations harbor built-in sources of social instability. As we saw, capitalist production is not self-sustaining, but free rides on social reproduction, nature, political power, and expropriation; yet its orientation to endless accumulation threatens to destabilize these very conditions of its possibility. In the case of its ecological conditions, what is at risk are the natural processes that sustain life and provide the material inputs for social provisioning. In the case of its social-reproduction conditions, what is imperiled are the sociocultural processes that supply the solidary relations, affective dispositions, and value horizons that underpin social cooperation, while also furnishing the appropriately socialized and skilled human beings who constitute "labor." In the case of its political conditions, what is compromised are the public powers, both national and transnational, that guarantee property rights, enforce contracts, adjudicate disputes, quell anti-capitalist rebellions, and maintain the money supply. In the case of capital's reliance on expropriated wealth, what is endangered is the system's self-professed universalism—and hence its legitimacy—and the ability of its dominant classes to rule hegemonically through a mix that includes consent as well as force. In each of these cases, the system harbors a built-in tendency to self-destabilization. Failing to replenish or repair its hidden abodes, capital persistently devours the very supports on which it relies. Like a serpent that eats its own tail, it cannibalizes its own conditions of possibility.

Here, in Marx's language, are four "contradictions of capitalism"—the ecological, the social, the political, and the racial/imperial—each of which corresponds to a genre of cannibalization and embodies a "crisis tendency." Unlike the crisis tendencies stressed by Marx, however, these do not stem from contradictions internal to the capitalist economy. They are grounded, rather, in contradictions between the economic system and its background conditions of possibility—between production and reproduction, society and nature, economy and polity, exploitation and expropriation.[15] Their effect, as we have seen, is to incite a broad range of social struggles in capitalist society: not only class struggles, narrowly defined, at the point of production, but also boundary struggles over ecology, social reproduction, political power, and expropriation. Responses to the crisis tendencies inherent in capitalist society, those struggles are endemic to our expanded view of capitalism as an institutionalized societal order.

What sort of critique of capitalism follows from the conception sketched here, of capitalism as institutionalized societal order? Conceiving capital as a cannibal implies a multi-stranded form of critical reflection, much like that developed by Marx in *Capital.* As I read him, Marx interweaves a systems critique of capitalism's inherent tendency to (economic) crisis, a normative critique of its built-in dynamics of (class) domination, and a political critique of the potential for emancipatory social transformation inherent in its characteristic form of (class) struggle. The view I have outlined here calls for an analogous interweaving of critical strands, but the weave here is more complex, as each strand is internally multiple. The system-crisis critique includes not only the economic contradictions discussed by Marx, but also the four inter-realm contradictions discussed here, which destabilize the necessary background conditions for capital accumulation by jeopardizing social reproduction, ecology, political power, and ongoing expropriation. Likewise, the domination critique encompasses not only the (production-centered) forms of class domination analyzed by Marx, but also those of gender domination, political domination, the domination of nature, and racial/imperial domination. Finally, the political critique encompasses multiple sets of actors—classes, genders, status groups, "races," nations, and *demoi*—and vectors of struggle: not only class struggles, but also boundary struggles, over the separations of social, political, natural, and expropriable peripheralized zones from "the economy."

What counts as an anti-capitalist struggle is thus much broader than Marxists have traditionally supposed. As soon as we look behind the front story to the backstory, then all the indispensable background conditions for the exploitation of labor become foci of conflict in capitalist society—not just struggles between labor and capital at the point of production, but also boundary struggles over gender domination, ecology, racism, imperialism, and democracy. But, equally important, the latter now appear in another light: as struggles in, around, and (in some cases) against capitalism itself. Should they come to understand themselves in these terms, participants in these struggles could conceivably cooperate or unite. In that case, their emancipatory potential would consist in their capacity to envision new configurations, not "merely" of economy, but also of the relation of economy to society, nature, and polity. Reimagining the structural divisions that have historically constituted capitalist societies would then represent the major task of social actors and critical theorists who are committed to emancipation in the twenty-first century.

That agenda forms the heart and soul of this book. In the chapters that follow, I take a closer look at each of the four hidden abodes I have outlined here. Integrating structural analysis with historical reflection and political theorizing, I disclose the forms of cannibalization proper to each: the racial/imperial dynamics of capitalism's expropriation/exploitation division, which feed the glutton's hunger for populations it can punish with impunity (chapter 2); the gendered dynamics of its reproduction/production couple, which stamp the system as a guzzler of care (chapter 3); the eco-predatory dynamics of its nature/humanity antithesis, which puts our planetary home in capital's maw (chapter 4); and the drive to devour public power and butcher democracy, which is built into the system's signature division between economy and polity (chapter 5). The last two chapters explore what practical difference it makes to rethink capitalism as a cannibal: how that view changes our understandings of socialism (chapter 6) and of the COVID-19 pandemic (Epilogue).

2

Glutton for Punishment: Why Capitalism Is Structurally Racist

Capitalism has always been deeply entangled with racial oppression. That proposition clearly holds for the slave-based plantation capitalism of the seventeenth through nineteenth centuries. But it is equally true of the Jim Crow industrialized capitalism of the twentieth century. Nor can anyone reasonably doubt that racial oppression persists in the deindustrializing, subprime, mass-incarceration capitalism of the present era. Despite the clear differences between them, none of these forms of "really existing" capitalism was nonracial. In all of its incarnations to date, capitalist society has been entangled with racial oppression.

What is the nature of this entanglement? Is it contingent or structural? Did the link between capitalism and racism arise by chance, and could matters have in principle been otherwise? Or was capitalism primed from the get-go to divide populations by race? And what about today? Is racism hardwired into *contemporary* capitalism? Or is a nonracial capitalism finally possible now, in the twenty-first century?

These questions are by no means new. To the contrary, they form the heart of a profound but underappreciated stream of critical theorizing, known as Black Marxism. This tradition, which flourished from the 1930s through the 1980s, includes such towering figures as C. L. R. James, W. E. B. Du Bois, Eric Williams, Oliver Cromwell Cox, Stuart Hall, Walter Rodney, Angela Davis, Manning Marable, Barbara Fields, Robin D. G.

Kelley, and Cornel West.[1] Although their approaches diverged in specifics, each of these thinkers grappled deeply with the capitalism/racism nexus. At least through the 1980s, their reflections were at the forefront of what many now call critical race theory.[2]

Subsequently, however, the question of capitalism's entanglement with race dropped off the critical-theoretical agenda. With the waning of New Left radicalism and the collapse of really existing Communism, capitalism ceased to be viewed as a topic of serious interrogation in many quarters, while Marxism was increasingly rejected as *dépassé*. As a result, questions of race and racism were effectively ceded to thinkers working in the liberal and poststructuralist paradigms. Although those thinkers made some impressive contributions to mainstream and critical race theory, they did not attempt to clarify the relation between capitalism and racial oppression.

Today, however, a new generation of critical race theorists is reinvigorating that problematic. Comprising thinkers like Michael Dawson, Ruth Wilson Gilmore, Cedric Johnson, Barbara Ransby, and Keeanga-Yamahtta Taylor, this generation is reconsidering the relation between capitalism and racism anew, in light of twenty-first-century developments.[3] The reasons are not hard to discern. The concurrent rise of a new generation of militant anti-racist activists, on the one hand, and of an aggressively ethno-nationalist and alt-right, white-supremacist populism, on the other, has dramatically raised the stakes of critical race theory. Under these conditions, many now feel the need for a better understanding of what they are fighting. Many now appreciate, too, that the broader context for both those developments is a deepening crisis of contemporary capitalist society, a crisis that is simultaneously exacerbating and rendering more visible its characteristic forms of racial oppression. Finally, "capitalism" is no longer a taboo term, and Marxism is enjoying a revival. In this situation, the central questions of Black Marxism have again become pressing: Is capitalism *necessarily* racist? Can racial oppression be overcome within capitalist society?

Here, I will aim to advance this problematic by drawing on the enlarged view of capitalism developed in the previous chapter. The approach I propose scrambles the usual sharp oppositions between structure and history, necessity and chance, which obscure the full complexity of the relation between capitalism and racism. Contrary to the proponents of contingency, who hold that racism is not necessary to capitalism, I maintain that there does exist a structural basis for the system's persistent entanglement with racial oppression. That basis resides, as we have seen, in the system's reliance on two analytically distinct but practically entwined processes of capital accumulation, *exploitation* and *expropriation*. It is the separation of these two "exes," and their assignment to two different populations, that underpins racial oppression in capitalist society.

Against proponents of necessity, who insist that nonracial capitalism is impossible, however, I shall argue that capitalism's exploitation/expropriation nexus is not set in stone. Rather, it changes historically over the course of capitalist development, which can be viewed as a sequence of qualitatively different regimes of racialized accumulation. In each phase, a historically specific configuration of the two exes underpins a distinctive landscape of racialization. When we follow the sequence down to the present, we encounter something new: a form of capitalism that blurs the historic separation of exploitation from expropriation. No longer assigning them to two sharply demarcated populations, this form appears to be dissolving the structural basis for racial oppression that inhered in capitalist society for four hundred years. Yet racial oppression persists, I shall claim, in forms that are neither strictly necessary nor merely contingent. The result is a new set of puzzles for Black Marxist theory and anti-racist activism in the twenty-first century.

In this chapter, I develop this argument in three steps. First, I defend the thesis that capitalism harbors a structural basis for racial oppression given that it relies on expropriation as a necessary condition for exploitation. Then, I historicize that structure by sketching the shifting configurations of those two exes in the principal phases of capitalism's history. Finally, I consider the prospects for overcoming racial oppression in a new form of capitalist society that still rests on exploitation and expropriation but does not assign them to two sharply demarcated populations. Throughout, I disclose the system's inherent tendency to racialize populations in order to better cannibalize them—and therefore, why we should understand capitalism as a glutton for their punishment.

Exchange, Exploitation, Expropriation

Is capitalism *necessarily* racist? Everything depends on what exactly is meant by "capitalism"—and on the perspective from which we conceive it. Three such perspectives are worth exploring. A first approach, taught in economics courses, assumed in business, and enshrined in common sense, views capitalism through the lens of market exchange. A second, familiar to socialists, trade unionists, and other protagonists of labor struggles, locates the crux of capitalism at a deeper level, in the exploitation of wage labor in commodity production. A third perspective, developed by critics of imperialism, puts the spotlight instead on capital's expropriation of conquered peoples. Here, I suggest that by combining the second and third perspectives we gain access to what is missed by each of the three approaches considered alone: a structural basis in capitalist society for racial oppression.

Consider, first, the perspective of exchange. From this perspective, capitalism appears as an economic system simpliciter. Organized to maximize growth and efficiency, it is centered on the institution of the market, where self-interested, arms-length transactors exchange equivalents. Seen this way, capitalism can only be indifferent to color. Absent interference and left to follow its own economizing logic, the system would dissolve any preexisting racial hierarchies and avoid generating any new ones. From the standpoint of exchange, the link between racism and capitalism is wholly contingent.

Much could be said about this view, but what is important for my present purposes is this: it de-links capitalism from racism by definitional fiat. By defining capitalism narrowly, as an inherently colorblind, utility-maximizing logic, the exchange-centered view relegates any racializing impulses to forces external to the market, which distort the latter's operation. The culprit is, therefore, not (what it understands as) capitalism, but the larger society that surrounds it. Racism comes from history, politics, and culture, all of which are viewed as external to capitalism and as only contingently connected to it. The effect is to formalize capitalism, reducing it to a means/end economizing logic and stripping away its historical and political contents. In this way, the market-centered view obscures the crucial point elaborated in chapter 1 and central to my argument here: for structural reasons, capitalist economies require "non-economic" preconditions and inputs, including some that generate racial oppression. By failing to reckon with that dependence, this view obfuscates the system's distinctive mechanisms of accumulation, domination, and cannibalization.

Some of those mechanisms are disclosed, by contrast, by our second perspective. Broader, less formal, and far less rosy, this view was originated by Karl Marx, who reconceived capitalism as a system of exploitation. Famously, he penetrated beneath the standard perspective of market exchange to the more fundamental level of commodity production. There he claimed to discover the secret of accumulation in capital's exploitation of wage laborers. For Marx, as we saw in the previous chapter, capitalism's workers are neither serfs nor slaves, but legally free individuals, free, that is, to enter the labor market and sell their "labor power." In reality, of course, they have little actual choice in the matter; deprived of any direct access to the means of production, they can only secure the means of subsistence by contracting to work for a capitalist in exchange for wages. Nor does the transaction redound to their benefit. What from the first perspective is an exchange of equivalents is in Marx's view a sleight of hand. Recompensed only for the average socially necessary cost of their own reproduction, capitalism's workers have no claim on the surplus value their labor generates, which accrues instead to the capitalist. And that is precisely the point. The crux of the system, for Marx, is exploitation, viewed as a relation between two classes: on the one hand, the capitalists who own the society's means of production and appropriate its surplus; on the other, the free but propertyless producers who must sell their labor power piecemeal in order to live. Capitalism, in Marx's view, is no mere economy, but a social system of class domination, centered on the exploitation of free labor by capital in commodity production.

Marx's perspective has many virtues, at least one of which is incontestable. By viewing capitalism through the lens of exploitation, it makes visible what the exchange perspective obscured: the structural basis in capitalist society for the class domination of (doubly) free workers. Yet this focus fails to disclose any comparable structural basis for racial oppression. On this point, at least, the exploitation perspective sits uncomfortably close to that of exchange. While demonstrating that capital is accumulated off the back of free waged labor, it sheds little if any light on how race figures in the system and why it plays such an outsize role in capitalism's history. Failing to address that issue, it can only convey the impression that the system's entanglement with racial oppression is contingent.

However, that conclusion is too hasty. The trouble is that in focusing so tightly on the process by which capital exploits wage labor, Marx failed to give systematic consideration to some equally fundamental processes that are bound up with exploitation. I have in mind two such processes that could, when probed, reveal deep-seated links to racial oppression. The first is the crucial role played in capital accumulation by unfree, dependent, and unwaged labor—by which I mean labor that is expropriated, as opposed to exploited, subject to domination unmediated by a wage contract. The second concerns the role of political orders in conferring the status of free individuals and citizens on "workers," while constituting others as lesser beings—for example, as chattel slaves, indentured servants, colonized subjects, "native" members of "domestic dependent nations," debt peons, "illegals," and felons.[4]

Both these matters—dependent labor and political subjection—come into view, however, when we take up a third perspective on capitalism: the standpoint of expropriation. Developed by theorists of imperialism, this way of thinking about capitalism, as noted in the previous chapter, broadens the frame beyond "the metropole" to encompass the conquest and looting of peoples in "the periphery." Adopting a global perspective, its practitioners disclose a hidden barbaric underside of capitalist modernity: beneath surface niceties of consent and contract lie brute violence and overt theft. The effect is to cast a new light on exchange and exploitation, which now appear as the tip of a larger, more sinister iceberg.

The expropriation perspective is revelatory, to be sure. What is not so clear, however, is whether imperial expansion is structurally integral to capitalism, and if so, how the expropriation of dependent, subjugated peoples relates to the exploitation of (doubly) free workers. Nor do we get a systematic account of what, if anything, this third "ex"—expropriation—has to do with racial oppression.

My claim is that expropriation is indeed integral to capitalist society—and to its entanglement with racism. In a nutshell, as I shall explain, the subjection of those whom capital *expropriates* is a hidden condition of possibility for the freedom of those whom it *exploits*. Absent an account of the first, we cannot fully understand the second. Nor can we glimpse the structural basis of capitalism's historic entanglement with racial oppression.

To unpack this claim, I will use the expanded conception of capitalism introduced in chapter 1, which combines elements of the last two perspectives canvased here. Penetrating beneath the familiar level of exchange, it combines Marx's "hidden abode" of *exploitation* with the even more obfuscated moment of *expropriation*. By theorizing the relation between those two exes, I shall identify a structural basis of capitalism's persistent entanglement with racial oppression.

Expropriation as Accumulation: The Economic Argument

Let me begin by expanding upon my definition of expropriation as a structuring element of capitalism. As we saw in the previous chapter, expropriation is accumulation by other means—other, that is, than exploitation. Dispensing with the contractual relation through which capital purchases "labor power" in exchange for wages, expropriation works by *confiscating* human capacities and natural resources and *conscripting* them into the circuits of capital expansion. The confiscation may be blatant and violent, as in New World slavery; or it may be veiled by a cloak of commerce, as in the predatory loans and debt foreclosures of the present era. The expropriated subjects may be rural or indigenous communities in the capitalist periphery—or members of subject or subordinated groups in the capitalist core. Once expropriated, these groups may end up as exploited proletarians, if they're lucky—or, if not, as paupers, slum dwellers, sharecroppers, "natives," or slaves, subjects of ongoing expropriation outside the wage contract. The confiscated assets may be labor, land, animals, tools, or mineral or energy deposits—but also human beings, their sexual and reproductive capacities, their children and bodily organs. What is essential, however, is that the commandeered capacities get incorporated into the value-expanding process that defines capital. Simple theft is not enough. Unlike the sort of pillaging that long predated the rise of capitalism, expropriation in the sense I intend here is *confiscation-cum-conscription-into-accumulation.*

Expropriation in this sense covers a multitude of sins, most of which correlate strongly with racial oppression. The association is clear in practices widely associated with capitalism's early history (though still ongoing), such as territorial conquest, land annexation, enslavement, coerced labor, child abduction, and systematic rape. But expropriation also assumes more "modern" forms—such as prison labor, transnational sex trafficking, corporate land grabs, and foreclosures on predatory debt, which are also linked with racial oppression—and, as we shall see, with contemporary imperialism.

However, the connection is not just historical and contingent. On the contrary, there are structural reasons for capital's ongoing recourse to racialized expropriation. By definition, a system devoted to the limitless expansion and private appropriation of surplus value gives the owners of capital a deep-seated interest in confiscating labor and means of production from subject populations. Expropriation raises their profits by lowering costs of production in two ways: on the one hand, by supplying cheap inputs, such as energy and raw materials; and on the other, by providing low-cost means of subsistence, such as food and textiles, which permit them to pay lower wages. Thus, by confiscating resources and capacities from unfree or dependent subjects, capitalists can more profitably exploit (doubly) free workers. Thus, the two exes are intertwined. Behind Manchester stands Mississippi.[5]

Advantageous even in "normal" times, expropriation becomes especially appealing in periods of economic crisis, when it serves as a critical, if temporary, fix for restoring declining profitability. The same is true for political crises, which can sometimes be defused or averted by transferring wealth confiscated from populations that appear not to threaten capital to those that do—another distinction that often correlates with "race."[6]

In general, then, expropriation is a structural feature of capitalism—and a disavowed enabling condition for exploitation. Far from representing separate and parallel processes, the two exes are systemically imbricated—deeply intertwined aspects of a single capitalist world system. And the division between them correlates roughly but unmistakably with what Du Bois called "the color line." All told, the expropriation of racialized "others" constitutes a necessary background condition for the exploitation of "workers."

Let me clarify this idea by contrasting it with Marx's account of "primitive" or "original" accumulation,[7] from which it differs in two respects. First, "primitive accumulation" denotes the blood-soaked process by which capital was initially stockpiled at the system's beginnings.[8] Expropriation, in contrast, designates an *ongoing* confiscatory process essential for sustaining accumulation in a crisis-prone system. Second, Marx introduces primitive accumulation to explain the historical genesis of the class division between propertyless workers and capitalist owners of the means of production. Expropriation explains that as well, but it also brings into view another social division, equally structural and consequential, but not systematically theorized by Marx: the social division between the (doubly) free workers (whom capital exploits in wage labor) and the unfree or dependent subjects (whom it cannibalizes by other means).

This second division is central to the present inquiry. My thesis is that the racializing dynamics of capitalist society are crystallized in the structurally grounded "mark" that distinguishes *free subjects of exploitation* from *dependent subjects of expropriation*. But to make this case requires a shift in focus —from "the economic" to "the political." For it is only by thematizing the *political orders* of capitalist society that we can grasp the constitution of that distinction—and with it, the fabrication of "race."

Expropriation as Subjection: The Political Argument

The distinction between expropriation and exploitation is simultaneously economic and political. Viewed economically, these terms name mechanisms of capital accumulation, analytically distinct yet intertwined ways of expanding value. Viewed politically, they have to do with modes of domination—especially with status hierarchies that distinguish rights-bearing individuals and citizens from subject peoples, unfree chattel, and dependent members of subordinated groups. In capitalist society, as Marx insisted, exploited workers have the legal status of free individuals, authorized to sell their labor power in return for wages. Once separated from the means of production and proletarianized, they are protected, at least in theory, from (further) expropriation. In this respect, their status differs sharply from those whose labor, property, and/or persons are *still* subject to confiscation on the part of capital. Far from enjoying political protection, the latter populations are rendered defenseless, fair game for expropriation—again and again. Thus, they are constituted as inherently violable. Deprived of the means to set limits to what others can do to them, their condition is one of exposure—to the most punishing forms of cannibalization.

In general, then, the distinction between expropriation and exploitation is a function not only of accumulation but also of domination. It is *political* agencies—above all, states—that afford or deny protection in capitalist society. And it is largely states, too, that codify and enforce the status hierarchies that distinguish citizens from subjects, nationals from aliens, and entitled workers from dependent scroungers. Constructing exploitable and expropriable subjects, while distinguishing the one from the other, state practices of political subjectivation supply an indispensable precondition for capital's "self"-expansion.[9]

Nevertheless, states do not act alone in this regard. Geopolitical arrangements are implicated as well. What enables political subjectivation at the national level is an international system that "recognizes" states and authorizes the border controls that distinguish lawful residents from "illegal aliens." We need only think of current conflicts surrounding migrants and refugees to see how easily these geopolitically enabled hierarchies of political status become racially coded.

The same is true of another set of status hierarchies, rooted in capitalism's imperialist geography, which divides the world into "core" and "periphery." Historically, the core has appeared to be the emblematic heartland of exploitation, while the periphery was cast as the iconic site of expropriation. That division was explicitly racialized from the get-go, as were the status hierarchies associated with it: metropolitan citizens versus colonial subjects, free individuals versus slaves, "Europeans" versus "natives," "whites" versus "blacks." These hierarchies, too, serve to distinguish populations and regions suitable for exploitation from those destined instead for expropriation.

To see how, let us look more closely at political subjectivation—especially at the processes that mark off (doubly) free, exploitable citizen-workers from dependent, expropriable subjects. Both these statuses were politically constituted, but in different ways. In the capitalist core, dispossessed artisans, farmers, and tenants became exploitable citizen-workers through historic processes of class compromise, which channeled their struggles for emancipation onto paths convergent with the interests of capital, within the liberal legal frameworks of national states. By contrast, those who became ever-expropriable subjects, whether in periphery or core, found no such accommodation, as their uprisings were more often crushed by force of arms. If the domination of the first was shrouded in consent and legality, that of the second rested unabashedly on naked repression.

Often, moreover, the two statuses were mutually constituted, effectively co-defining one another. In the United States, the status of the citizen-worker acquired much of the aura of freedom that legitimates exploitation by contrast to the dependent, degraded condition of chattel slaves and indigenous peoples, whose persons and lands could be repeatedly confiscated with impunity.[10] In codifying the subject status of the second, the US state simultaneously constructed the normative status of the first.

As noted above, however, the political fabrication of dependent subjects within capitalism has always exceeded state borders. For systemic reasons, rooted in the intertwined logics of geopolitical rivalry and economic expansionism, powerful states moved to constitute expropriable subjects further afield, in peripheral zones of the capitalist world system. Plundering the furthest reaches of the globe, European colonial powers, followed by a US imperial state, turned billions of people into such subjects—shorn of political protection, ripe and ready for confiscation. The number of expropriable subjects those states created far exceeds the number of citizen-workers they "emancipated" for exploitation. Nor did the process cease with the liberation of subject peoples from colonial rule. On the contrary, masses of new expropriable subjects are created daily, even now, by the joint operations of postcolonial states, their ex-colonial masters, and the trans-state powers that grease the machinery of accumulation—including the global financial institutions that promote dispossession by debt.

The common thread here, once again, is political exposure: the incapacity to set limits and invoke protections. Exposure is, in fact, the deepest meaning of expropriability, the thing that sets it apart from exploitability. And it is expropriability, the condition of being defenseless and liable to violation, that constitutes the core of racial oppression. Thus, what distinguishes free subjects of exploitation from dependent subjects of expropriation is the mark of "race" as a sign of violability.

My claim, to this point, is that capitalism harbors a structural basis for racial oppression. That basis is obscured when we view the system too narrowly, whether from the standpoint of market exchange or from that of the exploitation of free waged labor. The culprit appears, however, when the frame is broadened to include the third ex of expropriation, understood as a necessary condition for exploitation, distinct from but entwined with the latter. By adopting an enlarged perspective on capitalism that encompasses "politics" as well as "economics," we gain access to the system's noncontingent reliance on a stratum of unfree or subjugated people, racially marked as inherently violable. There, in capitalism's constitutive separation of exploitation from expropriation, lies the structural basis for its persistent entanglement with racial oppression.

Historical Regimes of Racialized Accumulation

Nevertheless, the structure I have described is susceptible to variation. Far from being given once and for all at capitalism's beginnings, it has undergone several major shifts in the course of capitalist development. In some phases, exploitation and expropriation were clearly separated from one another, with exploitation centered in the European core and reserved for the (white male) "labor aristocracy," while expropriation was sited chiefly in the periphery and imposed on people of color. In other phases, by contrast, those separations blurred. Such shifts have periodically reshaped the dynamics of racial oppression in capitalist society, which cannot be understood in abstraction from them. In effect, the relation between capitalism and racism is not only structural but also historical.

To clarify this double condition, I sketch an account of capitalism's history as a sequence of regimes of racialized accumulation. Here, in the second step of my argument, I foreground the historically specific relations between expropriation and exploitation within each principal phase of capitalist development. For each regime, I specify the geography and demography of the two exes: the extent to which they are separated from one another, sited in different regions, and assigned to distinct populations. For each regime, too, I note the relative weight of the two exes and the distinctive ways in which they are interconnected. Finally, I identify the forms of political subjectivation that characterize every phase.

I begin with the commercial or mercantile capitalism of the sixteenth through the eighteenth centuries. This was the era that Marx had in mind when he coined the phrase "primitive accumulation." With that phrase, he was signaling that the principal driver of accumulation in this phase of capitalism was not exploitation, but expropriation. Confiscation was the name of the game, manifested both in the land enclosures of the core and in the conquest, plunder, and "commercial hunting of black skins" throughout the periphery,[11] both of which long preceded the rise of modern industry. Prior to large-scale exploitation of factory workers came massive expropriation of bodies, labor, land, and mineral wealth in Europe and—especially—in Africa and the "New World." Expropriation literally dwarfed exploitation in commercial capitalism—and that had major implications for status hierarchy.

Certainly, this regime generated precursors of the racializing subjectivations that became so consequential in later phases: "Europeans" versus "natives," free individuals versus chattel, "whites" versus "blacks." But these distinctions were far less sharp in an era when virtually all non-propertied people had the status of subjects, not that of rights-bearing citizens. In this period, virtually *all* lacked political protection from expropriation, and the majority condition was not freedom but dependency. As a result, that latter status did not carry the special stigma it acquired in subsequent phases of capitalism, when majority-ethnicity male workers in the core won liberal rights through political struggle. It was only later, with the democratization of metropolitan states and the rise of large-scale factory-based exploitation of doubly free wage labor, that the contrast between "free and subject races" sharpened, giving rise to the full-blown white-supremacist status order we associate with modern capitalism.[12]

That is precisely what happened when mercantile capitalism gave way in the nineteenth century to liberal-colonial capitalism. In this new regime, the two exes became more balanced and interconnected. Certainly, the confiscation of land and labor continued apace, as European states consolidated colonial rule overseas, while the United States dispossessed natives at home and perpetuated its "internal colony," first through the extension of racialized slavery and then, after abolition, by transforming freedmen into debt peons through the sharecropping system. Now, however, ongoing expropriation in the periphery entwined with highly profitable exploitation in the core. What was new was the rise of large-scale factory-based manufacturing, which forged the proletariat imagined by Marx, upending traditional life forms and sparking widespread class conflict. Eventually, struggles to democratize metropolitan states delivered a system-conforming version of citizenship to exploited workers. At the same time, however, brutal repression of anti-colonial struggles ensured continuing subjection in the periphery. Thus, the contrast between dependency and freedom was sharpened and increasingly racialized, mapped onto two categorically different "races" of human beings. In this way, the free "white" exploitable citizen-worker emerged as the flip side of its own abjected enabling condition: the dependent racialized expropriable subject. And modern racism found a durable anchor in the deep structure of capitalist society.

Racialization was further strengthened by the apparent separation of expropriation and exploitation in the liberal-colonial regime. In this phase, the two exes appeared to be sited in different regions and assigned to different populations—one enslaved or colonized, the other (doubly) free. In fact, however, the division was never so clear cut, as some extractive industries employed colonial subjects in wage labor, and only a minority of exploited workers in the capitalist core succeeded in escaping ongoing expropriation altogether. Despite their appearance as separate, moreover, the two exes were systemically imbricated: it was the expropriation of populations in the periphery (including in the periphery within the core) that supplied the cheap food, textiles, mineral ore, and energy without which the exploitation of metropolitan industrial workers would not have been profitable. In the liberal-colonial period, therefore, the two exes were distinct but mutually calibrated engines of accumulation within a single world capitalist system.

In the following era, the nexus of expropriation and exploitation mutated again. Begun in the interwar period, and consolidated following the Second World War, the new regime of state-managed capitalism softened the separation of the two exes without abolishing it. In this era, expropriation no longer precluded exploitation but combined directly with it—as in the segmented labor markets of the capitalist core. In those contexts, capital exacted a confiscatory premium from racialized workers, paying them less than "whites"—and less than the socially necessary costs of their reproduction. Here, accordingly, expropriation was articulated directly with exploitation, entering into the internal constitution of wage labor in the form of dualized pay scales.

African Americans were a case in point. Displaced by agricultural mechanization and flocking to northern cities, many joined the industrial proletariat, but chiefly as second-class workers, consigned to the dirtiest, most menial jobs. In this era, their exploitation was overlaid by expropriation, as capital failed to pay the full costs of their reproduction. What undergirded that arrangement was their continuing political subjection under Jim Crow. Throughout the era of state-managed capitalism, Black Americans were deprived of political protection, as segregation, disfranchisement, and countless other institutionalized humiliations continued to deny them full citizenship. Even when employed in northern factories or western shipyards, they were still constituted as more or less expropriable, not as fully free bearers of rights. They were thus expropriated and exploited simultaneously.[13]

Even as it muddied the line between the two exes, the state-capitalist regime heightened the status differential associated with them. Newly created welfare states in the capitalist core lent additional symbolic and material value to the status of the citizen-worker, as they expanded protections and benefits for those who could claim them. Instituting labor rights, corporatist bargaining, and social insurance, they not only stabilized accumulation to capital's benefit but also politically incorporated those "workers" who were "merely" exploited. The effect, however, was to intensify the invidious comparison with those excluded from that designation, further stigmatizing racialized "others." Conspicuously anomalous and experienced as unjust, the latter's continuing vulnerability to violation became the target of sustained militant protest in the 1960s, as civil rights and Black Power activists took to the streets.

In the offshore periphery, meanwhile, struggles for decolonization exploded, giving rise in due course to a different amalgamation of the two exes. Independence promised to raise the status of ex-colonials from dependent subjects to rights-bearing citizens. In the event, some working-class strata did manage to achieve that elevation, but precariously and on inferior terms. In a global economy premised on unequal exchange, their exploitation, too, was suffused with expropriation, as trade regimes tilted against them siphoned value away to the core, notwithstanding the overthrow of colonial rule. Moreover, the limited advances enjoyed by some were denied to the vast majority, who remained outside the wage nexus and subject to overt confiscation. Now, however, the expropriators were not only foreign governments and transnational firms but also postcolonial states. Centered largely on import substitution industrialization, the latter's development strategies often entailed expropriation of "their own" indigenous populations. And even those developmental states that made serious efforts to improve the condition of peasants and workers could not fully succeed. The combination of straitened state resources, neo-imperial regimes of investment and trade, and ongoing land dispossession ensured that the line between the two exes would remain fuzzy in the postcolony.

In state-managed capitalism, therefore, exploitation no longer appeared so separate from expropriation. Rather, the two exes became internally articulated in racialized industrial labor, on the one hand, and in compromised postcolonial citizenship, on the other. Nevertheless, the distinction between the two exes did not disappear, as "pure" variants of each persisted in core and periphery. Substantial populations were still expropriated, pure and simple; and they were almost invariably people of color. Others were "merely" exploited; and they were more likely to be European and "white." What was new, however, was the emergence of hybrid cases in which some people were subject simultaneously to both expropriation and exploitation. Such people remained a minority under state-managed capitalism, but they were the heralds of a world to come.

When we turn to the present regime, we see a vast expansion of the expropriation/exploitation hybrid. This phase, which I'll call financialized capitalism, rests on a novel and distinctive nexus. On the one hand, there has been a dramatic shift in the geography and demography of the two exes. Much large-scale industrial exploitation now occurs outside the historic core, in the so-called BRICS[14] countries that once formed the semi-periphery. At the same time, expropriation is on the rise—so much so, in fact, that it threatens to once again outpace exploitation as a source of profit. These developments are closely connected. As industry migrates and finance metastasizes, expropriation is becoming universalized, afflicting not only its traditional subjects but also those who were previously shielded by their status as citizen-workers and free individuals.

Debt is a major culprit here, as global financial institutions pressure states to collude with investors in the cannibalization of wealth from defenseless populations. Indeed, it is largely by means of debt that peasants are dispossessed and corporate land grabs are intensified in the capitalist periphery. However, they are not the only victims. Virtually *all* non-propertied postcolonials are expropriated via sovereign debt, as postcolonial states in hock to international lenders and caught in the vise of "structural adjustment" are forced to abandon developmentalism in favor of liberalizing policies, which transfer wealth to corporate capital and global finance. Far from reducing debt, moreover, such restructuring only compounds it, sending the ratio of debt service to gross national product soaring skyward and condemning countless generations to expropriation, some long before they are born, and regardless of whether or not they are also subject to exploitation.

It is increasingly by expropriation, too, that accumulation proceeds in the historic core. As low-waged precarious service work replaces unionized industrial labor, wages fall below the socially necessary costs of reproduction. Workers who used to be "merely" exploited are now expropriated too. That double condition, previously reserved for minorities but increasingly generalized, is compounded by the assault on the welfare state. The social wage declines, as tax revenues previously dedicated to public infrastructure and social entitlements are diverted to debt service and "deficit reduction" in hopes of placating "the markets." Even as real wages plummet, services that used to be provided publicly, like childcare, are off-loaded onto families and communities—which is to say, chiefly onto women, who are meanwhile employed in precarious wage work, and hence exploited and expropriated coming and going. In the core, moreover, as in the periphery, a race to the bottom drives down corporate taxes, further depleting state coffers and apparently justifying more "austerity"—in effect, completing the vicious circle. Additional corporate giveaways eviscerate hard-won labor rights, setting up once-protected workers for violation. Yet they, like others, are expected to buy cheap stuff made elsewhere. Under these conditions, continued consumer spending requires expanded consumer debt, which fattens investors while cannibalizing citizen-workers of every color, but especially racialized borrowers, who are steered to hyper-expropriative subprime and payday loans. At every level and in every region, therefore, debt is the engine driving major new waves of expropriation in financialized capitalism.

In the present regime, then, we encounter a new entwinement of exploitation and expropriation—and a new logic of political subjectivation. In place of the earlier, sharp divide between dependent expropriable subjects and free exploitable workers, there appears a continuum. At one end lies the growing mass of defenseless expropriable subjects; at the other, the dwindling ranks of protected citizen-workers, subject "only" to exploitation. At the center sits a new figure, formally free, but acutely vulnerable: the *expropriated-and-exploited citizen-worker*. No longer restricted to peripheral populations and racial minorities, this new figure is becoming the norm.

Nevertheless, the expropriation/exploitation continuum remains racialized. People of color are still disproportionately represented at the expropriative end of the spectrum, as we see in the United States. Black and brown Americans who had long been denied credit, confined to inferior segregated housing, and paid too little to accumulate savings were systematically targeted by purveyors of subprime loans and consequently experienced the highest rates of home foreclosures in the country. Likewise, minority towns and neighborhoods that have long been starved of public resources are hit especially hard by plant closures, which cost them not only jobs but also tax revenues—hence, funds for schools, hospitals, and basic infrastructure maintenance, leading eventually to debacles in places like Flint, Michigan, and the Lower Ninth Ward of New Orleans. Finally, Black men long subject to differential sentencing and harsh imprisonment, coerced labor and socially tolerated violence (including at the hands of police), are massively conscripted into what critical race theorists have termed the prison-industrial complex—caged in carceral institutions kept full to capacity by a "war on drugs" targeting possession of small amounts of crack cocaine and by disproportionately high rates of unemployment. Despite the shift in the ex/ex nexus, racism is alive and well in financialized capitalism, which is truly a glutton for punishment.

Is Capitalism *Still* Necessarily Racist?

What follows for the theory and practice of anti-racism? Does the present softening of the ex/ex division mean that the structure that underpinned four hundred years of capitalist racial oppression is finally dissolving? Is capitalism *no longer* necessarily racist? And if so, is the power of racism to divide populations dissolving as well?

The analysis presented here suggests the crumbling, if not the full demise, of what has served historically as racism's structural basis in capitalist society. From its origins to the present, capitalism has always required both expropriation and exploitation. In the past, however, it also required their mutual separation and assignment to two distinct populations, divided by the color line. Today, by contrast, that second requirement no longer holds. On the contrary, the present regime conscripts nearly all non-propertied adults into wage labor, but it pays the overwhelming majority less than the socially necessary costs of their reproduction. Reducing the "social wage" by dismantling public provision, it entangles the bulk of the non-propertied population in the tentacles of debt. Universalizing precarity, financialized capitalism exploits and expropriates nearly everyone simultaneously.

Nevertheless, racial oppression lives on in this phase of capitalism. People of color remain racialized and far more likely than others to be poor, unemployed, homeless, hungry, and sick; to be victimized by crime and predatory loans; to be incarcerated and sentenced to death; to be harassed and murdered by police; to be used as cannon fodder or sex slaves and turned into refugees or "collateral damage" in endless wars; to be dispossessed and forced to flee violence, poverty, and climate change–induced disasters, only to be confined in cages at borders or left to drown at sea.

Taken together, these developments present an analytic puzzle. On the one hand, financialized capitalism is dissolving the political-economic structure that underpinned racial oppression in previous regimes. On the other hand, it still harbors racial disparities and foments racial antagonisms. The question is, why? Why does racism outlive the disappearance of the sharp separation of the two exes? Why do those who now share the objective condition of exploitation-cum-expropriation not see themselves as fellow travelers in the same (leaky, unseaworthy) boat? Why do they not join together to oppose financialized capitalism's fuzzier nexus of expropriation and exploitation, which harms them all?

That such alliances appeared only rarely in earlier phases of capitalism's history is not surprising. Previously, the racialized separation of the two exes encouraged the (doubly) free "workers" of the capitalist core to dissociate their interests and aims from those of dependent subjects in the periphery—including the periphery within the core. As a result, what was understood as class struggle was all too easily disconnected from struggles against slavery, imperialism, and racism—when not posed directly against them. And the converse was sometimes true: movements aimed at overcoming racial oppression at times despaired of alliances with "labor" and on occasion even disdained them. The effect throughout capitalism's history was to weaken the forces of emancipation.

But that was then. What are the prospects for such alliances today, when racial oppression in capitalist society is no longer strictly "necessary"? The perspective outlined here suggests a mixed prognosis. Objectively, financialized capitalism has softened the mutual separation of the two exes, which underpinned racism in the past. Subjectively, however, the new configuration may actually aggravate racial antagonism—at least in the short run. When centuries of racialized stigma and violation meet capital's voracious need for subjects to exploit and expropriate, the result is intense insecurity and paranoia—hence, a desperate scramble for safety—and exacerbated racism.

Certainly, those who were previously shielded from (much) predation are less than eager to share its burdens now—and not simply because they are racists, although some of them are. It is also that they, too, have legitimate grievances, which come out in one way or another—as well they should. In the absence of a cross-racial movement to abolish a social system that imposes near-universal expropriation, their grievances find expression in the growing ranks of right-wing authoritarian populism. Those movements flourish today in virtually every country of capitalism's historic core—as well as in quite a few countries of the former periphery. They represent the entirely predictable response to the "progressive neoliberalism" of our times. The elites who embody that perspective cynically appeal to "fairness" while extending expropriation—asking those who were once protected from the worst by their standing as "whites" or "Europeans" to give up that favored status, embrace their growing precarity, and surrender to violation, all while funneling their assets to investors and offering them nothing in return but moral approval.[15]

In this context, the political prospects for a post-racial society are not so rosy, notwithstanding the possibility of a structural opening. Cross-racial alliances do not emerge spontaneously from the new, more blurred configuration of the two exes. On the contrary, in the viciously predatory world of financialized capitalism, racial antagonisms are on the rise. Today, when a nonracial capitalism might be possible in principle, it appears to be barred in practice thanks to a toxic combination of sedimented dispositions, exacerbated anxieties, and cynical manipulations.

Before we bemoan that fact, however, we should ask what exactly nonracial capitalism could mean under current conditions. In one interpretation, it would be a regime in which people of color were proportionately represented at the commanding heights of global finance and political might, on the one hand, and among the latter's expropriated-cum-exploited victims, on the other. Contemplation of this possibility should not provide much comfort to anti-racists, as it would mean continued worsening of the life conditions of the vast majority of people of color, among others. Oriented to parity within ballooning inequality, a nonracial capitalism of this type would lead at best to equal-opportunity cannibalization amid rising racial animosity.

The analysis developed here suggests the pressing need for a more radical transformation. Despite the claims of progressive neoliberals, racism cannot be defeated by equal-opportunity cannibalization—nor, contra ordinary liberals, by legal reform. By the same token, and *pace* Black nationalists, the antidote does not reside in enterprise zones, community control, or self-determination. Nor, as traditional socialists would have it, can an exclusive focus on exploitation emancipate racialized people—nor, indeed, working people of any color. On the contrary, as we have seen here, it is also necessary to target the expropriation to which exploitation is systemically tied. What is needed, in fact, is to overcome capitalism's stubborn nexus of expropriation and exploitation, to transform the overall matrix, to eradicate both of capitalism's exes by abolishing the larger system that generates their symbiosis.

To overcome racism today requires cross-racial alliances aimed at achieving that transformation. Although such alliances do not emerge automatically as a result of structural change, they may be constructed through sustained political effort. The sine qua non is a perspective that stresses the symbiosis of exploitation and expropriation in financialized capitalism. By disclosing their mutual imbrication, such a perspective suggests that neither ex can be overcome on its own. Their fate is tied together, as is that of the populations who were once so sharply divided and are now so uncomfortably close. Today, when the exploited are also the expropriated and vice versa, it might be possible, finally, to envision an alliance among them. Perhaps in blurring the line between the two exes, financialized capitalism is creating the material basis for their joint abolition. But it's nevertheless up to us to seize the day and turn a historical possibility into real historical force for emancipation.

Achieving that goal would not be easy in any case. But it is further complicated when we consider some additional structural features of capitalist society. As we saw in chapter 1, racialized expropriation is not the only deep-seated form of domination in that society. It shares that status, rather, with injustices grounded in the other hidden abodes we have identified —political, ecological, and social-reproductive—and is deeply entangled with them. To understand racism fully requires understanding them as well. I turn accordingly in the following chapter to the gendered forms of cannibalization arising from capitalism's structural separation of production from reproduction.

3

Care Guzzler: Why Social Reproduction Is a Major Site of Capitalist Crisis

If capital feeds on the wealth of racialized populations, it is also a guzzler of care.[1] That aspect of its cannibal nature finds expression today in widespread social exhaustion and time poverty —experiences that have a structural basis in social reality. The fact is, our social system is sapping energies needed to tend to families, maintain households, sustain communities, nourish friendships, build political networks, and forge solidarities. Often referred to as carework, these activities are indispensable to society: they replenish human beings, both daily and generationally, while also maintaining social bonds. In capitalist societies, moreover, they assure the supply of commodified labor power from which capital sucks surplus value. Without this work of social reproduction, as I shall call it, there could be no production or profit or capital; no economy or culture or state. Indeed, it is fair to say that no society, capitalist or otherwise, that systematically cannibalizes social reproduction can endure for long. Yet the present form of capitalism is doing just that: diverting the emotional and material resources that should be devoted to carework to other, inessential activities, which fatten corporate coffers while starving us. The result is a major crisis—not simply of care, but of social reproduction in the broadest sense.

Bad as this crisis is, it is but one manifestation of the larger feeding frenzy described in this book. In this period, capital is cannibalizing not just social reproduction but also public powers and political capacities, as well as the wealth of nature and of racialized populations. The result is a general crisis of our entire societal order, a crisis whose various strands intersect with and exacerbate one another. Yet current discussions focus chiefly on the economic or ecological aspects, neglecting social reproduction, despite its urgency and importance. Doubtless linked to sexism, this neglect blocks our ability to rise to the challenge. The "care" strand is so central to the broader crisis that none of the other strands can be properly understood in abstraction from it. However, the converse is also true: the crisis of social reproduction is not freestanding and cannot be adequately grasped on its own. How, then, should it be understood?

I propose to interpret the present "care crunch" as an acute expression of a social-reproductive contradiction inherent in capitalism. This formulation suggests two ideas. First, the current strains on care are not accidental, but have deep structural roots in our present societal order, which I have referred to in previous chapters as financialized capitalism. Nevertheless —and this is the second point—the present crisis of social reproduction indicates something rotten not only in the system's current form but in capitalist society per se. Not just neoliberalism, but capitalism itself must be transformed.

My claim, then, is that every form of capitalist society harbors a deep-seated social contradiction or crisis tendency: on the one hand, social reproduction is a necessary background condition for sustained capital accumulation; on the other, capitalism's drive to unlimited accumulation leads it to cannibalize the very social-reproductive activities on which it relies. This social contradiction of capitalism lies at the root of our so-called crisis of care. Although inherent in capitalism as such, it assumes a different and distinctive guise in every historically specific form of capitalist society. The care deficits we experience today are the form this contradiction takes in the current, financialized phase of capitalist development.

Free Riding on the Lifeworld

To see why, we need to expand our understanding of what counts as a contradiction of capitalism. Most analysts stress contradictions internal to the system's economy. At its heart, they say, lies a built-in tendency to self-destabilization, which expresses itself periodically in economic crises: in stock market crashes, boom-bust cycles, and wholesale depressions. This view is right, as far as it goes. But it fails to provide a full picture of capitalism's inherent contradictions because it overlooks a crucial feature of this social system: capital's drive to cannibalize wealth in zones beyond (or, as I've said, behind) the economic. That oversight is quickly remedied, however, when we adopt the expanded understanding of capitalism that was outlined in the previous chapters. Because it encompasses both the official economy and its non-economic background conditions, that view permits us to conceptualize, and criticize, capitalism's full range of contradictions—including those centered on social reproduction. Let me explain.

The capitalist economy relies on—one might say, free rides on—activities of provisioning, caregiving, and interaction that produce and maintain social bonds, although it accords them no monetized value and treats them as if they were free. Variously called "care," "affective labor," or "subjectivation," such activity forms capitalism's human subjects, sustaining them as embodied natural beings while also constituting them as social beings, forming their habitus and the cultural ethos in which they move. The work of birthing and socializing the young is central to this process, as is caring for the old, maintaining households, building communities and sustaining the shared meanings, affective dispositions and horizons of value that underpin social cooperation.

Understood broadly, in this way, social reproductive work is essential to every society. In capitalist societies, however, it assumes another, more specific function: to produce and replenish the classes whose labor power capital exploits to obtain surplus value. Ironically, then, carework produces the labor that the system calls "productive" but is itself deemed "unproductive." It is true, of course, that much, though not all, carework is located outside the value-accumulating circuits of the official economy—in homes and neighborhoods, civil society institutions, and public agencies. And relatively little of it produces value in the capitalist sense, even when it is done for pay. But regardless of where it is done and whether or not it is paid, social-reproductive activity is necessary to capitalism's functioning. Neither the waged work that is deemed productive nor the surplus value extracted from it could exist in the absence of carework. It is only thanks to housework, child-rearing, schooling, affective care, and a host of related activities that capital can obtain a workforce suitable in quality and quantity to its needs. Social reproduction is an indispensable precondition for economic production in a capitalist society.[2]

From at least the industrial era onward, however, capitalist societies have separated the work of social reproduction from that of economic production. Associating the first with women, and the second with men, they have enveloped reproductive activities in a cloud of sentiment, as if this work should be its own reward—or failing that, as if it need only be paid a pittance, unlike work done directly for capital, which is (in theory) paid a wage on which the worker can actually live. In this way, capitalist societies created an institutional basis for new, modern forms of women's subordination. Splitting off reproductive labor from the larger universe of human activities, in which women's work previously held a recognized place, they relegated it to a newly institutionalized domestic sphere where its social importance was obscured, shrouded in the mists of newly invented notions of femininity. And in this new world, where money became a primary medium of power, its being unpaid or underpaid sealed the matter: those who perform essential reproductive work are made structurally subordinate to those who earn living wages for surplus-value generating labor in the official economy, even as the work of the first is what enables the work of the second.

In general, then, capitalist societies separate social reproduction from economic production, associating the first with women, and obscuring its importance and worth. Paradoxically, however, they make their official economies dependent on the very same processes of social reproduction whose worth they disavow. This peculiar relation of *division*-cum-*dependence*-cum-*disavowal* is a recipe for *destabilization*. In fact, those four D-words encapsulate a contradiction: on the one hand, capitalist economic production is not self-sustaining but relies on social reproduction; on the other, its drive to unlimited accumulation threatens to destabilize the very reproductive processes and capacities that capital—and the rest of us—need. The effect over time, as we shall see, is periodically to jeopardize the necessary social conditions of the capitalist economy.

Here, in effect, is a "social contradiction" lodged deep in the institutional structure of capitalist society. Like the economic contradictions that Marxists have stressed, this one, too, grounds a crisis tendency. In this case, however, the trouble is not located "inside" the capitalist economy but at the border that separates (and connects) production and reproduction. Neither intra-economic nor intra-domestic, it sets up a clash *between* the respective normative grammars-cum-action logics of those two realms. Often, of course, the contradiction is muted, and the associated crisis tendency remains obscured. It becomes acute, however, when capital's drive to expanded accumulation becomes unmoored from its social bases and turns against them. When that happens the logic of economic production overrides that of social reproduction, destabilizing the very processes on which capital depends—compromising the social capacities, both domestic and public, that are needed to sustain accumulation over the long term. Destroying its own conditions of possibility, capital's accumulation dynamic mimics the ouroboros and eats its own tail.

Historical Bouts of Capitalist Care Guzzling

This social contradiction is proper to capitalism in general, inscribed in its DNA. But it assumes different forms in different phases of the system's development. In fact, the capitalist organization of social reproduction has undergone major historical shifts, often as a result of political contestation. Especially in periods of crisis, social actors struggle over the boundaries demarcating economy from society, production from reproduction, and work from family, and sometimes succeed in redrawing them. Such "boundary struggles," as I called them in chapter 1, are as central to capitalist societies as are the point-of-production struggles often privileged by leftists, with which they are intertwined. And the shifts these struggles produce mark epochal transformations.

A perspective that foregrounds these shifts can distinguish four regimes of social reproduction–cum–economic production in capitalism's history. These match the sequence of regimes of racialized accumulation surveyed in chapter 2, with which they intersect and overlap. Here, too, we encounter the mercantile-capitalist regime of the sixteenth through eighteenth centuries, the liberal-colonial regime of the nineteenth; the state-managed regime of the mid-twentieth, and the financialized capitalist regime of the present era. My focus here, however, is the work of social reproduction, how it is organized and where it is situated in each phase. Are the people who perform it positioned as family members, as (un- or underpaid) domestics working in private households, as employees of profit-making firms, as community activists and volunteers in civil society, or as salaried civil servants?

For each regime, these questions have received different answers. Thus, the social-reproductive conditions for economic production have assumed a different guise in every era. So too have the crisis phenomena through which capitalism's social contradiction becomes manifest. In each regime, finally, that contradiction has incited distinctive forms of social struggle —class struggles, to be sure, but also boundary struggles and, as we shall see, struggles for emancipation.

Colonization and Housewifization

Consider, first, the mercantile capitalist regime of the sixteenth through eighteenth centuries. In the emerging imperial-commercial core, this regime left the business of creating and maintaining social bonds pretty much as it had been before—sited in villages, households, and extended kin networks, regulated locally by custom and church, far removed from national state action and relatively untouched by the law of value. At the same time, however, this regime violently upended precapitalist social bonds in the periphery—looting peasantries, enslaving Africans, dispossessing indigenous peoples, all with callous disregard for niceties of family, community, and kin. The resistance that ensued represented a first phase of struggle over social reproduction in capitalism's history.

The massive assault on peripheral sociality continued under the so-called liberal capitalism of the nineteenth century, as European states consolidated colonial rule. But things in the metropole changed dramatically. In the early manufacturing centers of the capitalist core, industrialists dragooned women and children into factories and mines, eager for their cheap labor and reputed docility. Paid a pittance and made to work long hours in unhealthy conditions, these workers became icons of capital's disregard for the social relations and capacities that underpinned its productivity.[3] Here, accordingly, the imperatives of production and reproduction appeared to stand in direct contradiction with each other. The result was a crisis on at least two levels: on the one hand, a crisis of social reproduction among the poor and working classes, whose capacities for sustenance and replenishment were stretched to the breaking point; on the other, a moral panic among the middle classes, who were scandalized by what they understood as the destruction of the family and the de-sexing of proletarian women. So dire was this situation that even such astute critics as Marx and Engels mistook this early head-on conflict between economic production and social reproduction for the final word. Imagining that capitalism had entered its terminal crisis, they believed that as the system eviscerated the working-class family, it was also eradicating the basis of women's oppression.[4] But what actually happened was just the reverse: over time, capitalist societies found resources for managing this contradiction—in part by creating "the family" in its modern restricted form; by inventing new, intensified meanings of gender difference; and by modernizing male domination.

The process of adjustment began, in the European core, with protective legislation. The idea was to stabilize social reproduction by limiting the exploitation of women and children in factory labor.[5] Spearheaded by middle-class reformers in alliance with nascent workers' organizations, this "solution" reflected a complex amalgam of different motives. One aim, famously characterized by the economic historian and anthropologist Karl Polanyi, was to "defend society against economy" in an epochal battle that he named the "double movement," which pitted free-marketeers against social protectionists.[6] Another was to allay anxiety over "gender leveling." But these motives were also entwined with something else: an insistence on masculine authority over women and children, especially within the family.[7] As a result, the struggle to ensure the integrity of social reproduction became entangled with the defense of male domination.

Its intended effect, however, was to mute the social contradiction in the capitalist core—even as slavery and colonialism raised it to an extreme pitch in the periphery. Creating what feminist sociologist Maria Mies called "housewifization" as the flip side of colonization,[8] liberal-colonial capitalism elaborated a new gender imaginary of separate spheres. Figuring woman as "the angel in the home," its proponents sought to create stabilizing ballast for the volatility of the economy. The cutthroat world of production was to be flanked by a "haven in the heartless world."[9] As long as each side kept to its own designated sphere and served as the other's complement, the potential conflict between them would remain under wraps.

In reality, this "solution" proved rather shaky. Protective legislation could not ensure labor's reproduction when wages remained below the level needed to support a family; when crowded, pollution-enveloped tenements foreclosed privacy, compromised fertility, damaged health, and shortened lives; and when employment itself (if available at all) was subject to wild fluctuations due to bankruptcies, market crashes, and financial panics. Nor did such arrangements satisfy workers. Agitating for higher wages and better conditions, they formed trade unions, went on strike, and joined labor and socialist parties. Riven by increasingly sharp, broad-based class conflict, capitalism's future seemed anything but assured.

Separate spheres proved equally problematic. Poor, racialized, and working-class women were in no position to satisfy Victorian ideals of domesticity; if protective legislation mitigated their direct exploitation, it provided no material support or compensation for lost wages. Nor were those middle-class women who could conform to Victorian ideals always content with their situation, which combined material comfort and moral prestige with legal minority and institutionalized dependency. For both groups, the separate-spheres "solution" came largely at women's expense. But it also pitted them against one another—witness nineteenth-century struggles over prostitution, which aligned the philanthropic concerns of Victorian middle-class women against the material interests of their "fallen sisters."[10]

A different dynamic unfolded in the periphery. There, as extractive colonialism ravaged subjugated populations, neither separate spheres nor social protection enjoyed any currency. Far from seeking to protect indigenous relations of social reproduction, metropolitan powers actively promoted their destruction. Peasantries were looted and their communities wrecked to supply the cheap food, textiles, mineral ore, and energy without which the exploitation of metropolitan industrial workers would not have been profitable. In the Americas, meanwhile, enslaved women's reproductive capacities were violently seized and bent to planters' profit calculations, and their families were routinely torn apart as members were sold off separately to different owners, often across long distances.[11] Native children, too, were ripped from their communities, conscripted into missionary schools, and subjected to coercive disciplines of assimilation.[12] When rationalizations were needed, apologists could just as easily invoke the unnaturally empowered condition of indigenous women as the backward, patriarchal state of non-western gender relations. The latter justification served well in colonial India, where philanthropic British women found a public platform, urging "white men to save brown women from brown men."[13]

In both settings, periphery and core, feminist movements found themselves navigating a political minefield. Rejecting coverture and separate spheres, while demanding the right to vote, refuse sex, own property, enter into contracts, practice professions, and control their own wages, liberal feminists appeared to valorize the male-coded aspiration to autonomy over ideals of nurture figured as womanly. And on this point, if on little else, their socialist-feminist counterparts effectively agreed. Conceiving women's entry into wage labor as the route to emancipation, the latter, too, preferred the values associated with production to those connoted by reproduction. These gendered associations were ideological, to be sure, but behind them lay a deep intuition: that despite the new forms of domination it brought, capitalism's erosion of traditional kinship relations contained an emancipatory moment.

In this situation, feminists were caught in a double bind. Many found scant comfort on either side of Polanyi's double movement. Neither the pole of social protection, with its attachment to male domination, nor that of marketization, with its disregard of social reproduction, could serve them well. Able neither to simply reject nor fully embrace the liberal order, some sought to develop a third orientation, which they called emancipation. To the extent that feminists managed to credibly embody that term, they exploded the two-sided schema of Polanyi, effectively transforming it into a triple movement.[14] In this three-sided conflict, proponents of protection and of marketization clashed not only with one another, but also with partisans of emancipation: with feminists, to be sure, but also with socialists, abolitionists, and anti-colonialists, all of whom endeavored to play off the two Polanyian poles against each other, even while clashing among themselves.

However promising in theory, such a strategy was hard to implement. As long as efforts to "protect society from economy" were identified with the defense of gender hierarchy, feminist opposition to male domination could easily be read as an endorsement of the economic forces that were ravaging working-class and peripheral communities. These associations would prove surprisingly durable, long after liberal-colonial capitalism collapsed under the weight of its multiple contradictions, in the throes of inter-imperialist wars, economic depressions, and international financial chaos, and finally gave way in the mid-twentieth century to a new regime.

Fordism and the Family Wage

Enter state-managed capitalism. Emerging from the ashes of the Great Depression and the Second World War, this regime sought to defuse the contradiction between economic production and social reproduction in a wholly new way—by enlisting state power on the side of reproduction. Assuming some public responsibility for what came to be known as social welfare, the states of this era sought to counter the corrosive effects of exploitation and mass unemployment on social reproduction. This aim was embraced by the democratic welfare states of the capitalist core and the newly independent developmental states of the periphery alike—despite their unequal capacities for realizing it.

Once again, the motives were mixed. A stratum of enlightened elites had come to believe that capital's short-term interest in squeezing out maximum profits had to be subordinated to the longer-term requirements for sustaining accumulation over time. The creation of the state-managed regime was a matter of saving the capitalist system from its own self-destabilizing propensities—as well as from the specter of revolution in an era of mass mobilization. Productivity and profitability required the biopolitical cultivation of a healthy, educated workforce with a stake in the system, as opposed to a ragged revolutionary rabble.[15] Public investment in health care, schooling, childcare, and old-age pensions, supplemented by corporate provision, was perceived as a necessity in an era in which capitalist relations had penetrated social life to such an extent that the working classes no longer possessed the means to reproduce themselves on their own. In this situation, social reproduction had to be internalized, brought within the officially managed domain of the capitalist order.

That project dovetailed with the new problematic of economic "demand." Aiming to smooth out capitalism's endemic boom-bust cycles, economic reformers sought to ensure continuous growth by enabling workers in the capitalist core to do double duty as consumers. Accepting unionization (which brought higher wages) and public sector spending (which created jobs), policy makers now reinvented the household as a private space for the domestic consumption of mass-produced objects of daily use.[16] Linking the assembly line with working-class familial consumerism, on the one hand, and with state-supported reproduction, on the other, this Fordist model forged a novel synthesis of marketization and social protection—projects Polanyi had considered antithetical.

But it was above all the working classes—both women and men—who spearheaded the struggle for public provision; and they acted for reasons of their own. For them, the issue was full membership in society as democratic citizens—and hence, dignity, rights, and respectability, as well as security and material well-being, all of which were understood to require a stable family life. In embracing social democracy, then, working classes were also valorizing social reproduction against the all-consuming dynamism of economic production. In effect, they were voting for family, country, and lifeworld against factory, system, and machine. Unlike the protective legislation of the prior regime, the state-capitalist settlement resulted from a class compromise and represented a democratic advance. Unlike its predecessor, too, the new arrangements served, at least for some and for a while, to stabilize social reproduction. For majority-ethnicity workers in the capitalist core, they eased material pressures on family life and fostered political incorporation.

But before we rush to proclaim a golden age, we should register the constitutive exclusions that made these achievements possible. As before, the defense of social reproduction in the core was entangled with (neo)imperialism. Fordist regimes financed social entitlements in part by ongoing expropriation from the periphery—including the "periphery within the core"—which persisted in old and new forms after decolonization.[17] Meanwhile, postcolonial states caught in the crosshairs of the Cold War directed the bulk of their resources, already depleted by imperial predation, to large-scale development projects, which often entailed expropriation of "their own" indigenous peoples. Social reproduction, for the vast majority in the periphery, remained outside the purview of governance, as rural populations were left to fend for themselves. Like its predecessor, too, the state-managed regime was entangled with racial hierarchy, as we saw in chapter 2. Social insurance in the United States excluded domestic and agricultural workers, effectively cutting off many African Americans from social entitlements.[18] And the racial division of reproductive labor, begun during slavery, assumed a new guise under Jim Crow, as women of color found low-paid waged work raising the children and cleaning the homes of "white" families—at the expense of their own.[19] Then, too, as we'll see in chapter 4, the state-managed regime rested on a new industrial-energic complex, centered on the internal combustion engine and refined oil. The effect was to base social-reproduction gains in the Global North on massive ecological damages—especially, but not only, in the Global South.

Nor was gender hierarchy absent from these arrangements. In a period—roughly from the 1930s to the end of the 1950s—when feminist movements did not enjoy much public visibility, hardly anyone contested the view that working-class dignity required "the family wage," male authority in the household, and a robust sense of gender difference. As a result, the broad tendency of state-managed capitalism in the countries of the core was to valorize the heteronormative male-breadwinner/female-homemaker model of the gendered family. Public investment in social reproduction reinforced these norms. In the United States, the welfare system took a dualized form, divided into stigmatized poor relief for (mostly "white") women and children lacking access to a male wage, on the one hand, and respectable social insurance for those (mostly "white" men) constructed as "workers," on the other.[20] By contrast, European arrangements entrenched androcentric hierarchy differently, in the division between mothers' pensions and entitlements tied to waged work—driven in many cases by pro-natalist agendas born of interstate competition.[21] Both models validated, assumed, and encouraged the family wage. Institutionalizing androcentric understandings of family and work, they naturalized heteronormativity, gender binarism, and gender hierarchy, largely removing the associated inequalities from political contestation.

In all these respects, social democracy sacrificed emancipation to an alliance of social protection and marketization, even as it mitigated capitalism's social contradiction for several decades. But the state-capitalist regime began unraveling; first politically, in the 1960s, when the global New Left erupted to challenge its imperial, gender, and racial exclusions, as well as its bureaucratic paternalism, in the name of emancipation; and then economically, in the 1970s, when stagflation, the "productivity crisis," and declining profit rates in manufacturing galvanized neoliberal efforts to unshackle marketization. What would be sacrificed, were those two parties to join forces, would be social protection.

Two-earner Households

Like the liberal-colonial regime before it, the state-managed capitalist order dissolved in the course of a protracted crisis. By the 1980s, prescient observers could discern the emerging outlines of a new regime, which would become the financialized capitalism of the present era. Globalizing and neoliberal, this regime promotes state and corporate disinvestment from social welfare while heavily recruiting women into the paid workforce—externalizing carework onto families and communities while diminishing their capacity to perform it. The result is a new, dualized organization of social reproduction, commodified for those who can pay for it and privatized for those who cannot, as some in the second category provide carework in return for (low) wages for those in the first. Meanwhile, the one-two punch of feminist critique and deindustrialization has definitively stripped the family wage of all credibility. That social-democratic ideal has given way to today's neoliberal norm of the "two-earner family."

The major driver of these developments, and the defining feature of this regime, is the new centrality of debt. As we will see in chapter 5, debt is the instrument by which global financial institutions pressure states to slash social spending, enforce austerity, and generally collude with investors in extracting value from defenseless populations. It is largely through debt, too, that peasants in the Global South are expropriated—dispossessed by a new round of corporate land grabs, aimed at cornering supplies of energy, water, arable land, and "carbon offsets." It is increasingly via debt as well that accumulation proceeds in the historic core: as low-waged, precarious service work replaces unionized industrial labor, wages fall below the socially necessary costs of reproduction; in this "gig economy," continued consumer spending requires expanded consumer credit, which grows exponentially.[22] It is increasingly through debt, in other words, that capital now cannibalizes labor, disciplines states, transfers wealth from periphery to core, and sucks value from households, families, communities, and nature.

The effect is to intensify capitalism's inherent contradiction between economic production and social reproduction. Whereas the previous regime empowered states to subordinate the short-term interests of private firms to the long-term objective of sustained accumulation, in part by stabilizing reproduction through public provision, this one authorizes finance capital to discipline states and publics in the immediate interests of private investors, not least by demanding public disinvestment from social reproduction. And whereas the previous regime allied marketization with social protection against emancipation, this one generates an even more perverse configuration in which emancipation joins with marketization to undermine social protection.

The new regime emerged from the fateful intersection of two sets of struggles. One set pitted an ascending party of free marketeers, bent on liberalizing and globalizing the capitalist economy, against declining labor movements in the countries of the core; once the most powerful base of support for social democracy, these latter are now on the defensive, if not wholly defeated. The other set of struggles pitted progressive "new social movements," opposed to hierarchies of gender, sex, "race," ethnicity, and religion, against populations seeking to defend established lifeworlds and (modest) privileges, now threatened by the "cosmopolitanism" of the new economy. Out of the collision of these two sets of struggles emerged a surprising result: a *progressive neoliberalism*, which celebrates "diversity," meritocracy, and "emancipation" while dismantling social protections and re-externalizing social reproduction. The effect is not only to abandon defenseless populations to capital's predations, but also to redefine emancipation in market terms.[23]

Emancipatory movements participated in this process. All of them—including anti-racism, multiculturalism, LGBTQ liberation, and environmentalism—spawned market-friendly neoliberal currents. But the feminist trajectory proved especially fateful, given capitalism's long-standing entanglement of gender and social reproduction. Like each of its predecessor regimes, financialized capitalism institutionalizes the production/reproduction division on a gendered basis. Unlike its predecessors, however, its dominant imaginary is liberal individualist and gender egalitarian: women are supposed to be the equals of men in every sphere, deserving of equal opportunities to realize their talents, including—perhaps especially—in the sphere of production. Reproduction, by contrast, appears as a backward residue, an obstacle to advancement that must be sloughed off, one way or another, en route to liberation.

Despite, or perhaps because of, its feminist aura, this liberal ideology epitomizes the current form of capitalism's social contradiction, which assumes a new intensity. As well as diminishing public provision and recruiting women into waged work, financialized capitalism has reduced real wages, thus raising the number of hours of paid work per household needed to support a family and prompting a desperate scramble to transfer carework to others.[24] To fill the care gap, the regime imports migrant workers from poorer to richer countries. Typically, it is racialized, often rural women from poor regions who take on the reproductive and caring labor previously performed by more privileged women. But to do this, the migrants must transfer their own familial and community responsibilities to other, still-poorer caregivers, who must in turn do the same—and on and on, in ever-longer global care chains. Far from filling the care gap, the net effect is to displace it—from richer to poorer families, from the Global North to the Global South.[25] This scenario fits the gendered strategies of cash-strapped, indebted postcolonial states subjected to the structural adjustment programs of the International Monetary Fund. Desperate for hard currency, some of them have actively promoted women's emigration to perform paid carework abroad for the sake of remittances, while others have courted foreign direct investment by creating export-processing zones, often in industries, such as textiles and electronics assembly, that prefer to employ women workers.[26] In both cases, social-reproductive capacities are further squeezed.

Two recent developments in the United States epitomize the severity of the situation. The first is the rising popularity of egg freezing, normally a $10,000 procedure, but now offered free by IT firms as a fringe benefit for highly qualified, well-paid female employees. Eager to attract and retain these workers, firms like Apple and Facebook provide them with a strong incentive to postpone childbearing, saying, in effect: "Wait and have your kids in your forties, fifties, or even sixties; devote your high-energy, productive years to us."[27] A second US development is equally symptomatic of the contradiction between reproduction and production: the proliferation of expensive, high-tech, mechanical pumps for expressing breast milk. This is the fix of choice in a country with a high rate of female labor force participation, no mandated paid maternity or parental leave, and a love affair with technology. This is a country, too, in which breastfeeding is de rigueur but has changed beyond all recognition. No longer a matter of suckling a child at one's breast, one "breastfeeds" now by expressing one's milk mechanically and storing it for feeding by bottle later by one's nanny. In a context of severe time poverty, double-cup, hands-free pumps are considered the most desirable, as they permit one to express milk from both breasts at once while driving to work on the freeway.[28]

Given pressures like these, is it any wonder that struggles over social reproduction have exploded in recent years? Northern feminists often describe their focus as the "balance between family and work."[29] But struggles over social reproduction encompass much more: community movements for housing, healthcare, food security, an unconditional basic income, and a living wage; struggles for the rights of migrants, domestic workers, and public employees; campaigns to unionize service-sector workers in for-profit nursing homes, hospitals, and childcare centers; and struggles for public services such as day care and elder care, for a shorter working week, and for generous paid maternity and parental leave. Taken together, these claims are tantamount to the demand for a massive reorganization of the relation between production and reproduction: for social arrangements that could enable people of every class, gender, sexuality, and color to combine social-reproductive activities with safe, interesting, and well-remunerated work.

Boundary struggles over social reproduction are as central to the present conjuncture as are (narrowly defined) class struggles over economic production. They respond, above all, to a "crisis of care" that is rooted in the structural dynamics of financialized capitalism. Globalizing and propelled by debt, this capitalism systematically cannibalizes the capacities available for sustaining social connections. Proclaiming the new ideal of the two-earner family, it recuperates movements for emancipation, which join with proponents of marketization to oppose the partisans of social protection, now turned increasingly resentful and chauvinistic.

Another Capitalism—or a New Socialist Feminism?

What might emerge from this crisis? Capitalist society has reinvented itself several times in the course of its history. Especially in moments of general crisis, when multiple contradictions —political, economic, ecological, and social reproductive— converge, boundary struggles have erupted at the sites of capitalism's constitutive institutional divisions: where economy meets polity, where society meets nature, where expropriation meets exploitation, and where production meets reproduction. At those boundaries, social actors have mobilized to redraw the institutional map of capitalist society. Their efforts propelled the shift, first, from the mercantile capitalism of the early modern era to the liberal-colonial capitalism of the nineteenth century, then to the state-managed capitalism of the twentieth, and finally to the financialized capitalism of the present era. Historically, too, capitalism's social contradiction has formed an important strand of the precipitating crisis, as the boundary dividing social reproduction from economic production has emerged as a major site and stake of struggle. In each case the gender order of capitalist society has been contested, and the outcome has depended on alliances forged among the principal poles of a triple movement: marketization, social protection, emancipation. Those dynamics propelled the shift, first, from separate spheres to the family wage, and then to the two-earner family.

What follows for the current conjuncture? Are the present contradictions of financialized capitalism severe enough to qualify as a general crisis, and should we anticipate another major mutation of capitalist society? Will the current crisis galvanize struggles of sufficient breadth and vision to transform the present regime? Might a new form of socialist feminism succeed in breaking up the mainstream movement's love affair with marketization, while forging a new alliance between emancipation and social protection—and if so, to what end? How might the reproduction/production division be reinvented today, and what can replace the two-earner family?

Nothing I have said here serves directly to answer these questions. But in laying the groundwork that permits us to pose them, I have sought to clarify the structural and historical underpinnings of the present conjuncture. I have suggested, specifically, that the roots of today's "crisis of care" lie in capitalism's inherent social contradiction—or rather in the acute form that contradiction assumes today, in financialized capitalism. If that is right, then this crisis will not be resolved by tinkering with social policy. The path to its resolution can only go through deep structural transformation of this societal order. What is required, above all, is to overcome financialized capitalism's rapacious subjugation of reproduction to production—but this time without sacrificing either emancipation or social protection. And that means reinventing the production/reproduction distinction and reimagining the gender order. It remains to be seen whether the result will be compatible with capitalism at all.

It remains to be seen, too, whether and how we can envision a new societal order that nourishes social reproduction without cannibalizing nature. That issue is front and center in the following chapter.

4

Nature in the Maw: Why Ecopolitics Must Be Trans-environmental and Anti-capitalist

Climate politics has moved to center stage. Even as pockets of denialism persist, political actors of multiple hues are turning green. A new generation of activist youth is insisting we face the mortal threat posed by global warming. Chastising elders for stealing their future, these militants claim the right and responsibility to take all necessary steps to save the planet. At the same time, movements for degrowth are gaining strength. Convinced that consumerist lifestyles are driving us into the abyss, they seek a transformation of ways of living. Likewise, indigenous communities, North and South, win expanded support for struggles only lately recognized as ecological. Long engaged in the defense of their habitats, livelihoods, and ways of life from colonial invasion and corporate extractivism, they find new allies today among those seeking noninstrumental ways of relating to nature. Feminists, too, are infusing new urgency into long-held ecological concerns. Positing psycho-historical links between gynophobia and contempt for the earth, they advocate forms of life that sustain reproduction—both social and natural. Meanwhile, a new wave of anti-racist activism includes environmental injustice among its targets. Adopting an expansive view of what it means to "defund the police," the Movement for Black Lives demands a massive redirection of resources to communities of color, in part to clean up toxic deposits that ravage health.

Even social democrats, lately complicit with or demoralized by neoliberalism, are finding new life in climate politics. Reinventing themselves as proponents of a Green New Deal, they aim to recoup lost working-class support by linking the shift to renewable energy with high-paying union jobs. Not to be left out, strands of right-wing populism are also greening. Embracing eco-national chauvinism, they propose to preserve "their own" green spaces and natural resources by excluding (racialized) "others." Forces in the Global South are also engaged on several fronts. While some claim a "right to development," insisting that the burden of mitigation should fall on Northern powers that have been spewing greenhouse gases for two hundred years, others advocate commoning or a social and solidary economy, while still others, donning the environmentalist mantle, utilize neoliberal carbon-offset schemes to enclose lands, dispossess those who live from them, and capture new forms of monopoly rent. Lest we forget, finally, corporate and financial interests have skin in the game. Profiting handsomely from booming speculation in eco-commodities, they are invested, not just economically but politically in ensuring the global climate regime remains market centered and capital friendly.

Ecopolitics, in a word, has become ubiquitous. No longer the exclusive property of stand-alone environmental movements, climate change now appears as a pressing matter on which every political actor must take a stand. Incorporated into a slew of competing agendas, the issue is variously inflected according to the differing commitments with which it keeps company. The result is a roiling dissensus beneath a superficial consensus. On the one hand, growing numbers of people now view global warming as a threat to life as we know it on planet Earth. On the other hand, they do not share a common view of the societal forces that drive that process—nor of the societal changes required to stop it. They agree (more or less) on the science but disagree (more than less) on the politics.

In reality, the terms "agree" and "disagree" are too pallid to capture the true situation. Present-day ecopolitics unfolds within, and is marked by, an epochal crisis. It is a crisis of ecology, to be sure, but also one of economy, society, politics, and public health—that is, a *general crisis* whose effects metastasize everywhere, shaking confidence in established worldviews and ruling elites. The result is a crisis of hegemony—and a wilding of public space. No longer tamed by a ruling common sense that forecloses out-of-the-box options, the political sphere is now the site of a frantic search not just for better policies, but for new political projects and ways of living. Gathering well before the COVID-19 outbreak, but greatly intensified by it, this unsettled atmosphere permeates ecopolitics, which perforce unfolds within it. Climate dissensus is fraught, accordingly, not "only" because the fate of the earth hangs in the balance, nor "only" because time is short, but also because the political climate, too, is wracked by turbulence.

In this situation, safeguarding the planet requires building a counterhegemony. What is needed, in other words, is to resolve the present cacophony of opinion into an ecopolitical common sense that can orient a broadly shared project of transformation. Certainly, such a common sense must cut through the mass of conflicting views and identify exactly what in society must be changed to stop global warming—effectively linking the authoritative findings of climate science to an equally authoritative account of the sociohistorical drivers of climate change. To become counterhegemonic, however, a new common sense must transcend the "merely environmental." Addressing the full extent of our general crisis, it must connect its ecological diagnosis to other vital concerns, including livelihood insecurity and the denial of labor rights; public disinvestment from social reproduction and the chronic undervaluation of carework; ethno-racial-imperial oppression and gender and sex domination; dispossession, expulsion, and exclusion of migrants; and militarization, political authoritarianism, and police brutality. Clearly, these concerns are intertwined with and exacerbated by climate change. But the new common sense must avoid reductive "ecologism." Far from treating global warming as a trump card that overrides everything else, it must trace that threat to underlying societal dynamics that also drive other strands of the present crisis. Only by addressing *all* major facets of this crisis, "environmental" and "non-environmental" alike, and by disclosing the connections among them, can we envision a counterhegemonic bloc that backs a common project and possesses the political heft to pursue it effectively.

This is a tall order, to be sure. But what brings it within the realm of the possible is a "happy coincidence": all roads lead to one idea—namely, capitalism. Capitalism, in the sense defined in previous chapters and extended in this one, represents the sociohistorical driver of climate change, and hence the core institutionalized dynamic that must be dismantled in order to stop it. But capitalism, so defined, is also deeply implicated in seemingly non-ecological forms of social injustice, from class exploitation to racial-imperial oppression and gender and sexual domination. And capitalism figures centrally, too, in seemingly non-ecological societal impasses: in crises of care and social reproduction; of finance, supply chains, wages, and work; of governance and de-democratization. Anti-capitalism, therefore, could—indeed *should*—become the central organizing motif of a new common sense. Disclosing the links among multiple strands of injustice and irrationality, it represents the key to the development of a powerful counterhegemonic project of eco-societal transformation.

That, at any rate, is the thesis I shall argue in this chapter. I develop it on three different levels. First, on the structural level, I contend that capitalism, rightly understood, harbors a deep-seated ecological contradiction, which inclines it to environmental crisis. But this contradiction is entwined with several others, equally endemic to capitalism, and cannot be adequately addressed in abstraction from them. Shifting, next, to the historical register, I chart the specific forms that capitalism's ecological contradiction has assumed in the various phases of the system's development, up to and including the present. Contra single-issue ecologism, this history discloses the pervasive entanglement of eco-crisis and eco-struggle with other strands of crisis and struggle, from which they have never been fully separable in capitalist societies. Turning, finally, to the political level, I contend that ecopolitics today must transcend the "merely environmental" by becoming anti-systemic across the board. Foregrounding global warming's entwinement with other pressing facets of our general crisis, I claim that green movements should turn *trans-environmental*, positioning themselves as participants in a broader counter-hegemonic bloc, centered on anti-capitalism, which could, at least in principle, save the planet.

Capitalism's Ecological Contradiction: A Structural Argument

What does it mean to say that capitalism is the principal socio-historical driver of global warming? At one level, this claim is empirical, a statement of cause and effect. Contrary to the usual vague references to "anthropogenic climate change," it pins the rap not on "humanity" in general but on the class of profit-driven entrepreneurs who engineered the fossil-fueled system of production and transport that released a flood of greenhouse gases into the atmosphere. That's a claim I shall defend empirically later on, when I turn to the historical portion of my argument. But there is more at work here than historical causality. Capitalism, as I understand it, drives global warming non-accidentally, by virtue of its very structure. It is this strong systematic claim, and not its weaker empirical cousin, that I unpack now.

I begin by preempting a possible misunderstanding. To say that capitalism drives climate change non-accidentally is *not* to say that ecological crises occur only in capitalist societies. On the contrary, many precapitalist societies have perished as a result of environmental impasses, including some of their own making—as when ancient empires ruined the farmlands on which they depended through deforestation or failure to rotate crops. Likewise, some self-proclaimed postcapitalist societies generated severe environmental damage through relentless quotidian coal-burning and spectacular one-off disasters such as Chernobyl. Such cases show that ecological devastation is not unique to capitalism.

What *is* unique, however, is the structural character of the link between ecological crisis and capitalist society. Precapitalist eco-crises occurred in spite of "nature-friendly" worldviews and largely thanks to ignorance—for example, the failure to anticipate the consequences of deforestation and overplanting. They could have been prevented—and sometimes were—by social learning that prompted shifts in social practice. Nothing in the inherent dynamics of these societies required the practices that spawned the damages. The same is true for self-proclaimed postcapitalist societies. "Really existing socialisms," paradigmatically the Soviet Union, practiced unsustainable agricultural and industrial regimens, poisoning the land with chemical fertilizers and fouling the air with CO_2. Unlike their precapitalist predecessors, of course, their practices aligned with worldviews that were not at all "nature friendly," and their actions were shaped by ideological commitments enjoining the "development of the productive forces." What is crucial, however, is that neither those worldviews nor those commitments arose from dynamics *internal* to socialism. Their roots lay, rather, in the geopolitical soil in which these socialisms germinated—in a world system structured by competition with capitalist societies, by the "catch-up" extractivist mindset that environment fostered, and by the fossil-fueled models of mega-industrialization it favored. To say this is not to let the rulers of these societies off the hook; they will remain forever culpable for disastrous decisions made in bureaucratic-authoritarian milieus saturated with fear and obsessed with secrecy—qualities they deliberately cultivated. The point is rather that nothing in the nature of socialist society requires such milieus or such decisions. Absent the prevailing external constraints and internal deformations, such societies could in principle develop sustainable patterns of interaction with nonhuman nature.

The same cannot be said for capitalist societies. They are unique among known social systems in entrenching a deep-seated tendency to ecological crisis at their very core. As I shall explain, capitalist societies are primed to generate recurrent environmental crises throughout their history. Unlike those of other societies, their ecological impasses cannot be resolved by increased knowledge or green bona fides. What is required is deep structural transformation.

To see why, we must revisit the concept of capitalism. As we've seen in previous chapters, capitalism is not an economic system but something bigger. More than a way of organizing economic production and exchange, it is also a way of organizing the *relation* of production and exchange to their *non-economic conditions of possibility*. It is well understood in many quarters that capitalist societies institutionalize a dedicated economic realm—the realm of a peculiar abstraction known as "value"—where commodities are produced on privately owned means of production by exploited wage laborers and sold on price-setting markets by private firms, all with the aim of generating profits and accumulating capital. What is often overlooked, however, is that this realm is constitutively dependent—one could say, parasitic—on a host of social activities, political capacities, and natural processes that are defined in capitalist societies as non-economic. Accorded no "value" and positioned outside it, these constitute the economy's indispensable presuppositions.

Certainly, as I argued in chapter 3, commodity production is inconceivable absent the unwaged activities of social reproduction that form and sustain the human beings who perform wage labor. Likewise, as we'll see in chapter 5, such production could not exist without the legal orders, repressive forces, and public goods that underpin private property and contractual exchange. Finally, as I'll explain in detail here, neither profit nor capital would be possible apart from the natural processes that assure availability of vital inputs, including raw materials and sources of energy. Essential conditions for a capitalist economy, these "non-economic" instances are not external to capitalism but integral elements of it. Conceptions of capitalism that omit them are ideological. To equate capitalism with its economy is to parrot the system's own economistic self-understanding, and thus to miss the chance to interrogate it critically. To gain a critical perspective, we must understand capitalism more broadly: as an institutionalized societal order that encompasses not only "the economy" but also those activities, relations, and processes, defined as non-economic, that make the economy possible.

What is gained from this revision is the ability to examine something crucial: *the relation established in capitalist societies between the economy and its "others"*—including that vital other known as "nature." At its core, this relation is contradictory and crisis prone. On the one hand, the system's economy is constitutively dependent on nature, both as a tap for production's inputs and as a sink for disposing its waste. At the same time, capitalist society institutes a stark division between the two "realms"—constructing economy as a field of creative human action that generates value, while positioning nature as a realm of stuff, devoid of value, but infinitely self-replenishing and generally available to be processed in commodity production.

This ontological gulf becomes a raging inferno when capital enters the mix. A monetized abstraction engineered to "self-expand," capital commands accumulation without end. The effect is to incentivize owners bent on maximizing profits to commandeer "nature's gifts" as cheaply as possible, if not wholly gratis, while also absolving them of any obligation to replenish what they take and repair what they damage. The damages are the flip side of the profits. With their ecological reproduction costs discounted, all the major inputs to capitalist production and circulation are vastly cheapened—not "just" raw materials, energy, and transport, but also labor, as wages fall with the cost of living when capital wrests foodstuffs from nature on the cheap. In every case, capitalists appropriate the savings in the form of profit, while passing the environmental costs to those who must live with—and die from—the fallout, including future generations of human beings.

More than a relation to labor, then, *capital is also a relation to nature*—a cannibalistic, extractive relation, which consumes ever more biophysical wealth in order to pile up ever more "value," while disavowing ecological "externalities." What also piles up, not accidentally, is an ever-growing mountain of eco-wreckage: an atmosphere flooded by carbon emissions; climbing temperatures, crumbling polar ice shelves, rising seas clogged with islands of plastic; mass extinctions, declining biodiversity, climate-driven migration of organisms and pathogens, increased zoonotic spillovers of deadly viruses; superstorms, megadroughts, giant locust swarms, jumbo wildfires, titanic flooding; dead zones, poisoned lands, unbreathable air. Systemically primed to free ride on a nature that cannot really self-replenish without limit, capitalism's economy is always on the verge of destabilizing its own ecological conditions of possibility.

Here, in effect, is an ecological contradiction lodged at the heart of capitalist society—in the relation this society establishes between economy and nature. Grounded deep in the system's structure, this contradiction is encapsulated in four words that begin with the letter *d*: dependence, division, disavowal, and destabilization. In a nutshell: capitalist society makes "economy" *depend* on "nature," while *dividing* them ontologically. Enjoining maximal accumulation of value, while defining nature as not partaking of it, this arrangement programs economy to *disavow* the ecological reproduction costs it generates. The effect, as those costs mount exponentially, is to *destabilize* ecosystems—and, periodically, to disrupt the entire jerry-rigged edifice of capitalist society. Simultaneously needing and rubbishing nature, capitalism is in this respect, too, a cannibal that devours its own vital organs. Like the ouroboros, it eats its own tail.[1]

The contradiction can also be formulated in terms of class power. By definition, capitalist societies devolve to capital, or, rather, to those dedicated to its accumulation, the task of organizing production. It is the class of capitalists whom this system licenses to extract raw materials, generate energy, determine land use, engineer food systems, bioprospect medicinals, and dispose of waste—effectively ceding to them the lion's share of control over air and water, soil and minerals, flora and fauna, forests and oceans, atmosphere and climate—which is to say, over all the basic conditions of life on earth. Capitalist societies thus vest a class that is strongly motivated to trash nature with the power to manage our relations with it.

Granted, governments sometimes intervene post hoc to mitigate the damages—but always reactively, in the mode of catch-up, and without disturbing the owners' prerogatives. Because they are always a step behind the emitters of greenhouse gases, environmental regulations are easily subverted by corporate workarounds. And because they leave intact the structural conditions that license private firms to organize production, they do not alter the fundamental fact: the system gives capitalists motive, means, and opportunity to savage the planet. It is they, and not humans in general, who have brought us global warming—but not by chance or simple greed. Rather, the dynamic that has governed their actions and led to that outcome is baked into the very structure of capitalist society.

Whichever formulation we start with, the conclusion we reach is the same: capitalistically organized societies carry an ecological contradiction in their DNA. They are primed to precipitate "natural catastrophes," which occur periodically, but not accidentally, throughout their history. Thus, these societies harbor a built-in tendency to ecological crisis. They generate ecosystemic vulnerabilities on an ongoing basis, as part and parcel of their modus operandi. Although not always acute or even apparent, the vulnerabilities pile up over time, until a tipping point is reached and the damage bursts forth into view.

Entangled Contradictions

To say that capitalism's ecological problem is structural is to say that we cannot save the planet without disabling some core, defining features of our societal order. What is needed, first and foremost, is to wrest the power to dictate our relation to nature away from the class that currently monopolizes it so that we can begin to reinvent that relation from the ground up. But that requires dismantling the system that underpins their power: the military forces and property forms, the pernicious ontology of "value" and the relentless dynamic of accumulation, all of which work together to drive global warming. Ecopolitics must, in sum, be anti-capitalist.

That conclusion is conceptually powerful as it stands. But it doesn't yet tell the whole story. To complete the picture, we need to consider some additional structural features of capitalist society that also impact nature and the struggles surrounding it. What is crucial here is a point I alluded to earlier: nature is neither the only non-economic background condition for a capitalist economy nor the only site of crisis in capitalist society. Rather, as already noted, capitalist production also relies on social-reproductive and political prerequisites. And these arrangements, too, are contradictory—no less than the arrangements surrounding nature. Equally important, they interact with the latter in ways we ignore at our peril. They, too, must be included in an ecocritical theory of capitalist society.

Consider the social-reproductive conditions for a capitalist society. Here, too, capitalism organizes more than just production. As I argued at length in chapter 3, it also structures the relations between production and the multiple forms of carework performed by communities and families—chiefly, but not only, by women. Sustaining the human beings who constitute "labor" and forging the social bonds that enable cooperation, carework is indispensable to any system of social provisioning. But capitalism's distinctive way of organizing it is every bit as contradictory as its way of organizing nature. Here, too, the system works through splitting—in this case, splitting production off from reproduction and treating the first alone as a locus of value. The effect is to license the economy to free ride on society, to cannibalize carework without replenishment, to deplete the energies needed to provide it, and thus to jeopardize an essential condition of its own possibility. Here, too, therefore, a tendency to crisis is lodged at the very heart of capitalist society—in this case, a tendency to social reproductive crisis.

An analogous contradiction dogs the relation in capitalist society between "the economic" and "the political." On the one hand, a capitalist economy necessarily relies on a host of political supports: on repressive forces that contain dissent and enforce order; on legal systems that guarantee private property and authorize accumulation; on multiple public goods that enable private firms to operate profitably. Absent these political conditions, a capitalist economy could not exist. But capitalism's way of relating economy to polity is also self-destabilizing. Splitting off the private power of capital from the public power of states, this arrangement incentivizes the first to hollow out the second. Firms whose raison d'être is endless accumulation have every reason to evade taxes, weaken regulation, privatize public goods, and offshore their operations—thus cannibalizing the political prerequisites for their own existence. Primed in this case, too, to devour its tail, capitalist society also harbors a deep-seated tendency to political crisis, which we'll explore in greater detail in the following chapter.

Here, then, are two further contradictions of capital, which also follow the four-D logic of division, dependence, disavowal, and destabilization. Considered in this light, as analytical abstractions, they closely parallel the ecological contradiction dissected here. But that formulation misleads. The three contradictions do not in fact operate in parallel but, rather, *interact* with one another—and with the economic contradictions diagnosed by Marx. In fact, the interactions among them are so intimate and mutually constitutive that none of them can be fully understood in isolation from the others.

Consider that the work of social reproduction is deeply concerned with matters of life and death. Care of children encompasses not only socialization, education, and emotional nurturance but also gestation, birthing, postnatal tending to bodies, and ongoing physical protection. Likewise, care for the sick and dying is focused on healing bodies and easing pain as well as on providing solace and assuring dignity. And everyone—young or old, sick or well—depends on carework to maintain shelter, nutrition, and sanitation for the sake of both physical well-being and social connection. In general, then, social reproductive work aims to sustain beings who are simultaneously natural and cultural. Confounding that distinction, it manages the interface of sociality and biology, community and habitat.

Social reproduction is thus intimately entangled with ecological reproduction, which is why so many crises of the first are also crises of the second—and why so many struggles over nature are also struggles over ways of life. When capital destabilizes the ecosystems that support human habitats, it simultaneously jeopardizes caregiving—as well as the livelihoods and social relations that sustain it. When people fight back, conversely, it is often to defend the entire ecosocial nexus at a single stroke, as if to defy the authority of capitalism's divisions. Ecocritical theorists should follow their example. We cannot adequately understand capitalism's ecological contradiction unless we think the latter together with its social-reproductive contradiction. Although the system works to separate both nature and care from economy, it simultaneously sets in motion extensive interactions among them. These interactions deserve a prominent place in the ecocritical theory of capitalist society.

The same point holds for the ecological and the political, which are also intimately linked in capitalist society. It is public powers, usually states, which supply the legal and military might that enables capital to expropriate natural wealth gratis or on the cheap. And it is to public powers that people turn when ecological damages become so immediately threatening that they can no longer be ignored. It is states, in other words, that capitalist societies task with policing the boundary between economy and nature: with promoting or restraining "development," with regulating or deregulating emissions; with deciding where to site toxic waste dumps, whether and how to mitigate their effects, whom to protect, and whom to place in harm's way.

Struggles over the relation between economy and nature are thus unavoidably political—in more than one sense. Typically focused on the concrete policies that states do or should pursue in order to protect nature from the economy, they often turn into conflicts over the limits of public power, its right and capacity to rein in private (corporate) power. Also at stake in such struggles is jurisdiction: the proper scale and agency for intervention in matters, such as global warming, that are by definition trans-territorial. Likewise at issue is the grammar of nature: the social meanings attributed to it, our place within it, and our relation to it. Finally, as we'll see in chapter 5, what looms behind every eco-contest is the all-important metapolitical question: Who, exactly, should determine these matters? At every level, therefore, the nature/economy nexus is political. We cannot understand the ecological dimension of capitalism's current crisis unless we grasp its interactions with the political strand. Nor can we hope to resolve the first without also resolving the second.

The ecological is also entangled, finally, with capitalism's constitutive division between exploitation and expropriation. As we saw in chapter 2, that division corresponds roughly to the global color line, marking off populations whose social reproduction costs capital absorbs, through the payment of living wages, from those whose labor and wealth it simply seizes with little if any compensation. Whereas the first are positioned as free, rights-bearing citizens, able to access (at least some level of) political protection, the second are constituted as dependent or unfree subjects, enslaved or colonized, unable to call on state protection and stripped of every means of self-defense. This distinction has always been central to capitalist development, from the era of New World racialized chattel slavery to that of direct-rule colonialism to postcolonial neo-imperialism and financialization. In each case, the expropriation of some has served as an enabling condition for the profitable exploitation of others. The disavowal of this setup is central to capitalism's own narrative and helps ensure its continuance.

Expropriation has also served as a method by which capital accesses energy and raw materials very cheaply, if not for free. The system develops in part by annexing chunks of nature for whose reproduction it does not pay. In appropriating nature, however, capital simultaneously expropriates human communities, for whom the confiscated material and befouled surroundings constitute a habitat, their means of livelihood, and the material basis of their social reproduction. These communities thus bear a hugely disproportionate share of the global environmental load; their expropriation affords other ("whiter") communities the chance to be sheltered, at least for a while, from the worst effects of capital's cannibalization of nature. The system's built-in tendency to ecological crisis is therefore tightly linked to its built-in tendency to create racially marked populations for expropriation. In this case too, ecocritical theory cannot adequately understand the first apart from the second.

All told, capitalism's ecological contradiction cannot be neatly separated from the system's other constitutive irrationalities and injustices. To ignore the latter by adopting the reductive ecologistic perspective of single-issue environmentalism is to miss the distinctive institutional structure of capitalist society. Dividing economy not only from nature but also from state, care, and racial/imperial expropriation, this society institutes a tangle of mutually interacting contradictions, which critical theory must track together, in a single frame.

That conclusion gains additional support when we shift our focus to history.

Three Ways of Talking about "Nature"

First, however, a word about "nature." Widely recognized as slippery, that term has appeared in the preceding pages in two different senses, which I now propose to disaggregate, before introducing a third. In speaking of global heating as a brute reality, I have assumed a conception of nature as the object studied by climate science: a nature that "bites back" when carbon sinks are flooded, operating via biophysical processes that proceed behind our backs, independently of whether or not we understand them. That scientific-realist conception, call it Nature I, is at odds with another meaning I've invoked to explain capitalism's ecological contradiction. "Nature" there was referenced from capital's viewpoint, as the ontological other of "Humanity": a collection of stuff, devoid of value, but self-replenishing and appropriable as means to the system end of value expansion. That conception, call it Nature II, is a construct of capitalism, historically specific to it but by no means a simple fiction or mere idea. Operationalized in the dynamic of capital accumulation, which also proceeds systemically, independently of our understanding, it has become a potent force with momentous practical consequences for Nature I. Much of my argument to this point has sought to illuminate the catastrophic hijacking of Nature I by Nature II in capitalist society.

Now, however, as we turn to history, we are poised to meet yet another conception of nature. This one, Nature III, is the object studied by historical materialism: concrete and changing over time, always already marked by prior metabolic interactions among its human and nonhuman elements. This is nature entangled with human history, shaped by and shaping the latter. We see it in the transformation of biodiverse prairies into monocultural farm lands; in the replacement of old-growth forests by tree plantations; in the destruction of rainforests to make way for mining and cattle ranching; in the preservation of "wilderness areas" and the reclamation of wetlands; in farmed animals and genetically modified seeds; in climate- and "development"-induced species migrations that trigger zoonotic spillovers of viruses—to cite examples from the (relatively short) capitalist phase of the earth's history. The eco-marxian thinker Jason W. Moore evokes the idea of Nature III when he proposes to replace the uppercase singular "Nature" with the lowercase plural "historical natures."[2] I shall use Moore's expression in what follows, along with the adjective "socioecological," to portray the society/nature interface as an interactive historical nexus—a nexus that capital has tried to control and now threatens to obliterate.

This third conception of nature, as inextricably entangled with human history, will be front and center in the following step of my argument, which situates capitalism's ecological contradiction historically. But that focus by no means excludes or invalidates Nature I or Nature II. Contra Moore, both of those conceptions are legitimate—and compatible with Nature III.[3] And both will find a place in my story—as objective historical forces that operate behind our backs and as (inter) subjective beliefs that motivate our actions. We'll see, too, that the beliefs collide not only with one another, but with other, subaltern understandings of nature that also possess the capacity to "bite back"—in this case, through social struggle and political action. In sum, we need all three conceptions of nature working in concert to chart the historical career of capitalism's ecological contradiction.

Socioecological Regimes of Accumulation

To this point, I have elaborated capitalism's tendency to ecological crisis in structural terms, as if it existed outside of time. In reality, however, this tendency finds expression only in historically specific forms, or, as I shall call them, "socioecological regimes of accumulation." I use that phrase to designate the various phases whose succession forms capitalism's history. Each regime represents a distinctive way of organizing the economy/nature relation. Each features characteristic methods of generating energy, extracting resources, and disposing of waste. Likewise, regimes exhibit distinctive trajectories of expansion—ways of annexing previously external chunks of nature through historically specific mixes of conquest, theft, commodification, nationalization, and financialization. Finally, regimes develop characteristic strategies for externalizing and managing nature: methods of off-loading damages onto families and communities that lack political clout and are deemed disposable; and schemes for distributing responsibility for mitigation among states, intergovernmental organizations, and markets. What makes a regime distinctive, then, is where it draws the line between economy and nature, and how it operationalizes that division. Equally important, as we shall see, are the concrete meanings a regime ascribes to nature—in both theory and practice.

None of these matters is given once and for all with the advent of capitalism. Rather, they shift historically, often in times of crisis. Those are times when the long-brewing effects of capitalism's ecological contradiction become so apparent, so insistent, that they can no longer be finessed or ignored. When that happens, the established organization of the economy/nature relation appears dysfunctional, unjust, unprofitable, or unsustainable and becomes subject to contestation. The effect is to incite broad struggles among rival political blocs with competing projects aimed at defending or transforming that relation. When they do not end in stalemate, such struggles may install a new socioecological regime. Once in place, the new regime provides provisional relief, overcoming at least some of its predecessor's impasses, while incubating new ones of its own, whose effects will become apparent later, as it matures. That outcome is guaranteed, alas, insofar as the new regime fails to overcome capitalism's built-in tendency to ecological crisis and merely defuses or displaces it, however creatively.

That, at any rate, is the scenario that has prevailed to date. As a result, capitalism's history can now be viewed as a sequence of socioecological regimes of accumulation, punctuated by regime-specific developmental crises, each of which is resolved provisionally by the successor regime, which in due course generates a developmental crisis of its own.[4] Later, we shall consider whether this sequence may now be coming to an end, thanks to a deeper dynamic that subtends it: namely, the epochal, trans-regime progression of global warming—

cumulatively escalating, seemingly implacable, and threatening to stop the whole show. Whatever we say about that, there is no denying that the economy/nature division has mutated several times in the course of capitalism's history, as has the organization of nature. My principal aim in this section is to chart these shifts and the crisis dynamics that drive them.

The historical career of capitalism's ecological contradiction spans the same four regimes of accumulation we encountered in previous chapters: the mercantile-capitalist phase of the sixteenth through eighteenth centuries; the liberal-colonial regime of the nineteenth and early twentieth; the state-managed phase of the second third of the twentieth century; and the current regime of financialized capitalism. In each of these phases, the economy/nature relation has assumed a different guise, as have the crisis phenomena generated by it. Each regime, too, has precipitated distinctive types of struggles over nature. Yet one thing has remained constant throughout: in each case, eco-crisis and eco-struggle have been deeply entwined with other strands of crisis and struggle, also grounded in structural contradictions of capitalist society.

Animal Muscle

I begin with mercantile capitalism—and with the question of energy. In that phase, as earlier, wind powered sailing ships, while windmills and watermills ground grain in some locales. But agriculture and manufacturing ran largely on animal muscle, both human and otherwise (oxen, horses, etc.), just as they had for millennia. Continuous in this respect with precapitalist societies, mercantile capitalism was what environmental historian J. R. McNeill calls a "somatic" regime: conversion of chemical into mechanical energy occurred mostly inside the bodies of living beings as they digested food, which originated from biomass.[5] And that meant that, as in earlier eras, the principal way to augment available energy was through conquest. Only by annexing land and commandeering additional supplies of labor could mercantile-capitalist powers increase their forces of production. As we saw in previous chapters, they made ample use of those time-tested methods, but on a vastly expanded scale that encompassed the "new" world as well as the "old."

In the periphery, then, mercantile-capitalist agents installed brutal systems of socioecological extractivism. From the silver mines of Potosí to the slave plantations of Saint-Domingue, they worked land and labor to the point of exhaustion, making no effort to replenish what they expended.[6] Electing instead to devour ever-new human and nonhuman "inputs" forcibly incorporated from "the outside," they left trails of environmental and social wreckage across whole continents. Those on the receiving end fought back with varying degrees of success. Aimed at countering wholesale assaults on habitats, communities, and livelihoods, their resistance was necessarily integrative. Whether communalist, counter-imperial, or republican, it combined what we would now call "environmental" struggles with struggles over labor, social reproduction, and political power.

In the metropole, meanwhile, capital scaled up by other means. Forcible land enclosures in England facilitated the conversion of farmland to sheep pasture, enabling expanded manufacture of textiles even in the absence of mechanization. That shift in land use and property regime converged with a major round of administrative state building in the sixteenth century—and with a world-changing scientific revolution in the seventeenth. The latter gave us the mechanical view of nature, an early version of Nature I that was instrumental in the creation of Nature II. Hardening distinctions inherited from Greek philosophy and Christianity, the mechanical view expelled nature from the cosmos of meaning, effectively replacing suppositions of socio-natural proximity with a deep ontological chasm. Objectified and externalized, Nature now appeared as Humanity's antithesis—a view that seemed to some to license its "rape."[7] As it turned out, philosophical ideas of this sort proved inessential to modern science and were eventually dropped from later versions of Nature I. But they found a second life in capital's metaphysic, which posited Nature II as inert and there for the taking.

In general, then, mercantile capitalism articulated conquest and extractivism in the periphery with dispossession and modern science in the core. We could say, with the benefit of hindsight, that in this era capital was amassing biotic and epistemic forces whose larger productive potential would only become apparent later, with the advent of a new socioecological regime of accumulation.

King Coal

That regime began to take shape in early nineteenth-century England, which pioneered the world-historic shift to fossil energy. James Watt's invention of the coal-fired steam engine opened the way to the world's first "exosomatic" regime: the first to take carbonized solar energy from beneath the crust of the earth and convert it to mechanical energy *outside of living bodies*. Because it was thus tied only indirectly to biomass, the liberal-colonial regime appeared to liberate the forces of production from the constraints of land and labor. At the same time, it called into being a new historical nature. Coal, previously of interest only locally as a substance to burn for heat, now became an internationally traded commodity. Extracted from confiscated lands and transported in bulk across long distances, energy deposits formed over hundreds of million years were consumed in the blink of an eye in order to power mechanized industry, without regard for replenishment or pollution. Equally important, fossilized energy provided capitalists with a means to reshape the relations of production to their advantage. In the 1820s and '30s, British textile manufacturers, reeling from strikes in the mills, shifted the bulk of their operations from place-bound hydropower to mobile steam—which also meant from country to city. In that way, they were able to tap concentrated supplies of proletarianized labor—workers with less access to means of subsistence and more tolerance for factory discipline than their rural counterparts.[8] Apparently, the cost of coal (which, unlike water, had to be bought) was outweighed by gains from intensified exploitation.

If coal-fired steam powered the industrial revolution in production, it also revolutionized transport. Railroads and steamships compressed space and quickened time, speeding the movement of raw materials and manufactures across great distances, and thus accelerating capital's turnover and swelling its profits.[9] The effects on agriculture were also profound. With hungry proletarians massed in the cities, there was money to be made from unsustainable, profit-driven farming in the countryside. But of course, that arrangement greatly exacerbated the metabolic rift between town and country. Nutrients plundered from rural soil were not returned at the point of extraction but discharged into urban waterways as organic waste. Thus, the coal-fueled liberal-colonial regime exhausted farmlands and polluted cities in a single stroke.[10]

This massive disruption of the soil nutrient cycle epitomized capitalism's ecological contradiction in its liberal-colonial phase. Equally emblematic was the response, as fixes purporting to solve Europe's soil-depletion crisis served only to displace or exacerbate it. One improbable but profitable undertaking centered on guano, scraped from steep rocky crags off the coast of Peru by semi-enslaved Chinese workers and shipped to Europe for sale as fertilizer—all to the principal benefit of English investors. One result was a series of anti- and inter-imperial wars for control of the trade.[11] Another, as deposits built up over centuries began to dwindle within a few decades, was the invention and wide use of chemical fertilizers, whose downstream effects include soil acidification, groundwater pollution, ocean dead zones, and rising levels of nitrous oxide in the atmosphere—all deeply inimical to humans and other animals.

There is also a further irony. Fossil-fueled production in the capitalist core expanded throughout the liberal-colonial era. But, as the guano gambit showed, the appearance of liberation from land and animal muscle was an illusion. Exosomatic industrialization in Europe, North America, and Japan rested on a hidden abode of somatic-based extractivism in the periphery. What made Manchester's factories hum was the massive import of "cheap natures"[12] wrested from colonized lands by masses of unfree and dependent labor: cheap cotton to feed the mills; cheap sugar, tobacco, coffee, and tea to stimulate the "hands"; cheap bird shit to feed the soil that fed the workers. Thus, the apparent savings of labor and land was actually a form of environmental load displacement—a shift in the demands placed on biomass from core to periphery.[13] Colonial powers ramped up the process by calculated efforts to wipe out manufacturing in their colonies. Deliberately destroying textile production in Egypt and India, Britain reduced those lands to suppliers of cotton for its mills and captive markets for its products.[14]

Theorists and historians of eco-imperialism are only now reckoning the full extent of this cost shifting,[15] while also revealing the close connection of anti-colonialism with proto-environmentalism. Rural struggles against liberal-colonial predation were also "environmentalisms of the poor," struggles for environmental justice avant la lettre.[16] They were struggles, too, over the meaning and worth of nature, as European imperialists raised on distanced scientific conceptions sought to subjugate communities that did not distinguish sharply between nature and culture.

In the capitalist core, where people *did* make that distinction, (proto-)environmentalism looked rather different. The most celebrated version conjured a "Nature" viewed, like the one fantasized by capital, as Humanity's Other, but figured as sublime and beyond price—and hence as demanding reverence and protection. The flip side of Nature II, this Nature was also ideological. But far from licensing extractivism, it fed Romantic-conservative critiques of industrial society. Originally pastoralist and backward looking, the natural sublime infused stand-alone "environmentalisms of the rich,"[17] which focused on wilderness preservation. Often thought to exhaust the whole of (proto-)environmentalism in this era, it coexisted in reality with another perspective—one that linked capital's assault on nature with class injustice. Key proponents of that perspective were William Morris, whose ecosocialism included a powerful aesthetic dimension, and Friedrich Engels, whose social environmentalism focused initially on industrialism's deleterious impact on urban working-class health and later on "the dialectics of nature"—or what we would now call co-evolutionism and biological emergentism. Both thinkers seeded rich traditions of socialist ecology that were subsequently obscured by narrow single-issue understandings of environmentalism but are now being recovered and extended.[18]

Age of the Automobile

But of course, liberal-colonial capitalism's chief legacy was not environmentalism, but the fateful world-changing shift to exosomatic energy, which "liberated" fossilized stores of carbon that had been safely sequestered beneath the earth's crust for many millennia. That legacy, which brought us global warming, was embraced and extended in the following era of state-managed capitalism, as a new global hegemon orchestrated a vast expansion in greenhouse gas emissions. The United States, having supplanted Britain, built a novel exosomatic-industrial complex around the internal combustion engine and refined oil. The result was the age of the automobile: icon of consumerist freedom, catalyst of highway construction, enabler of suburbanization, spewer of carbon dioxide, and reshaper of geopolitics. Thus, coal-fired "carbon democracy" gave way to an oil-fueled variant, courtesy of the United States.[19]

Refined oil also powered social democracy. Profits from auto and related manufactures supplied a sizeable chunk of the tax revenues that financed postwar social provision in wealthy countries. The irony went largely unnoticed: what underwrote increased public spending on social welfare in the Global North was intensified private plunder of nature in the Global South. Apparently, capital would foot the bill for some social reproduction costs here only if permitted to dodge a much larger bill for natural reproduction costs there.[20] The linchpin of the arrangement was oil, without which the whole operation would have ground to a halt. To guarantee supplies and control, the United States sponsored a raft of coups d'état in the Persian Gulf and Latin America, securing the profits and position of Big Oil and Big Fruit. The latter, like Big Food more generally, capitalized on the evolving technology of oil-guzzling, ozone-depleting refrigerated transport to regionalize an unsustainable industrialized food system, while further contaminating the atmosphere.[21] All told, oil-fueled social democracy at home rested on militarily imposed oligarchy abroad.[22]

At the same time, the United States also begat a powerful environmental movement. One current, descended from the nature-romanticism of the previous regime and originating in the nineteenth century, centered on wilderness protection through the creation of reserves and national parks, often by means of indigenous displacement.[23] "Progressive," as opposed to backward looking, this environmentalism of the rich was compensatory; aimed at enabling (some) Americans to escape industrial civilization temporarily, it neither confronted the latter nor sought to transform it. As state-managed capitalism developed, however, it hatched another environmentalism—one that targeted the industrial nucleus of the regime. Galvanized by biologist and conservationist Rachel Carson's 1962 book, *Silent Spring*, this current pushed for state action to curtail corporate pollution. The result was the creation of the Environmental Protection Agency, a parallel of sorts to the New Deal agencies that supported social reproduction. Founded in 1970 at the tail end of the state-managed era, the EPA was the regime's last major effort to defuse systemic crisis by "internalizing externalities" as objects of state regulation. The jewel in its crown was the Superfund, tasked with cleaning up toxic waste sites on US territory on capital's dime. Financed chiefly by taxes on the petroleum and chemical industries, the fund realized the principle of "polluter pays" through the coercive agency of the capitalist state, unlike current carbon trading schemes, which substitute the carrot for the stick and rely on markets.

However progressive in that respect, state-capitalist regulation of nature (like that of social reproduction) was built on disavowed cost shifting. It unloaded eco-"externalities" disproportionately onto poor communities in the core—especially, but not only, communities of color—while ramping up extractivism and environmental load displacement in the periphery. Moreover, US environmentalism's industrial wing misframed its central issue of corporate pollution. Positing the national-territorial state as the relevant unit for eco-policy, it failed to reckon with the inherently transborder character of industrial emissions.[24] That "oversight" would prove especially fateful with respect to greenhouse gases, whose effects are by definition planetary. Although the process was not fully understood at the time, the detonation of that ticking time bomb was hugely hastened, as the regime relentlessly cranked out CO_2 throughout its lifespan.

New Enclosures, Financialized Nature, and "Green Capitalism"

Today, in the era of financialized capitalism, all of these "bads" continue on steroids—though on an altered basis. Relocation of manufacturing to the Global South has scrambled the previous energic geography. Somatic and exosomatic formations now coexist side by side throughout Asia, Latin America, and some regions of southern Africa. The Global North, meanwhile, increasingly specializes in the "post-material" triad of IT, services, and finance—aka Google, Amazon, and Goldman Sachs. But once again, the appearance of liberation from nature is misleading. Northern "post-materialism" rests upon southern materialism (mining, agriculture, manufacturing)—as well as on fracking and offshore drilling in its own backyard. Equally important, consumption in the Global North is ever more carbon intensive: witness steep rises in air travel, meat eating, cement paving, and overall material throughput.

Meanwhile, capital continues to generate new historical natures at a rapid pace. These include new must-have minerals, such as lithium and coltan—the latter an essential ingredient of mobile phones, a Central African casus belli, and a super-profitable commodity mined in some instances by enslaved Congolese children. Other neoliberal natures are familiar objects newly enclosed. A prime example is water, whose privatization is fiercely resisted by populations intent on safeguarding not only their "material interests" but also "the source of life" and related subaltern views of the nature/community nexus.[25]

Although enclosures have been integral to every phase of capitalism, the current regime generates new forms that are as insidious as ingenious. Famously, cutting-edge biotech joins with state-of-the-art intellectual property law to engineer new types of monopoly rent. In some cases, Big Pharma claims ownership of indigenous plant-based medicinals, such as those derived from the Indian neem tree whose genome they lately decoded, despite the fact that the curative properties in question have been known and used for centuries throughout South Asia. Similarly, Big Agra seeks to patent crop strains, such as basmati rice, on the basis of notional genetic "improvements" in order to dispossess the farming communities that developed them. In other cases, by contrast, the expropriators bioengineer new historical natures that do not occur "in nature." A notorious example is Monsanto's Terminator seeds, deliberately designed to be sterile so that farmers must purchase them every year. Here, a multinational intentionally snuffs out the natural life-renewing process by which seeds are reproduced in order to engorge the artificial life-extinguishing process by which capital reproduces itself.[26] Effectively turning its own conception of Nature II upside down, capital now denies to others the use of that very "free gift" on which it itself has always relied: nature's capacity to self-replenish. The result is a tangle of super-profits and multiple miseries in which the environmental entwines with the social. Sharply rising peasant debt leads to waves of peasant suicides, further impoverishing regions already saddled with a growing share of the global environmental load: extreme pollution in cities, hyper-extractivism in the countryside, and disproportionate vulnerability to increasingly lethal impacts of global warming.

These asymmetries are compounded by new, financialized modes of regulation, premised on new, neoliberal conceptions of Nature II. With the delegitimation of public power comes the new/old idea that the market can serve as the principal mechanism of effective governance, now tasked with curtailing greenhouse gas emissions and saving the planet. But carbon trading schemes only draw capital away from the massive coordinated investment needed to de-fossilize the world's economy and transform its energic basis. Money flows instead into speculative trade in emissions permits, ecosystem services, carbon offsets, and environmental derivatives. What enables such "regulation," and is also fostered by it, is a new, green-capitalist imaginary that subjects the whole of nature to an abstract economizing logic, even when it does not directly commodify it. The idea that a coal-belching factory here can be "offset" by a tree plantation there assumes a nature composed of fungible, commensurable units whose place-specificity, qualitative traits, and experienced meanings can be disregarded.[27] The same is true for the hypothetical auction scenarios, beloved of environmental economists, that purport to assign value to a "natural asset" according to how much various actors would pay to realize their competing "preferences" regarding it: are indigenous communities sufficiently "invested" in the preservation of their local fishing stocks to outbid the corporate fleets that threaten to deplete them? If not, the rational use of the "asset" is to allow its commercial exploitation.[28] These green-capitalist scenarios represent a sophisticated new way of internalizing nature, which cranks epistemic abstraction up a notch, to the meta level. But some things never change. Like its predecessor variants of Nature II, financialized nature, too, is a vehicle of cannibalization.

Under these conditions, the grammar of ecopolitics is shifting. As global warming has displaced chemical pollution as the central issue, so have markets in emissions permits supplanted coercive state power as the go-to regulatory mechanism, and the international has replaced the national as the favored arena of eco-governance. Environmental activism has altered accordingly. The wilderness protection current has weakened and split, with one branch gravitating to the green-capitalist power center, the other to increasingly assertive movements for environmental justice. The latter rubric now encompasses a broad range of subaltern actors—from southern environmentalisms of the poor resisting enclosures and land grabs, to northern anti-racists targeting disparities in exposure to toxins, to indigenous movements fighting pipelines, to ecofeminists battling deforestation—many of which overlap and link to one another in transnational networks. At the same time, state-focused projects, lately sidelined, are now reemerging with new vigor. As populist revolts both left and right have shattered belief in the magical properties of "free markets," some are returning to the view that national state power can serve as the principal vehicle of eco-societal reform: witness Marine Le Pen's "New Ecology," on the one hand, and the Green New Deal, on the other. So too labor unions, long committed to defending the occupational health and safety of their members but wary of curbs on "development," now look to green infrastructure projects to create jobs. Finally, at the other end of the spectrum, degrowth currents find new recruits among youth attracted by their bold civilizational critique of spiraling material throughput and consumer lifestyles—and by the promise of "buen vivir" through veganism, commoning, and/or a social and solidary economy.

But what does all of this add up to, and where might it lead?

Nature Cannibalized in Space and Time

To this point, I've offered structural arguments and historical reflections in support of two propositions: first, that capitalism harbors a deep-seated ecological contradiction that inclines it non-accidentally to environmental crisis; and second, that those dynamics are entangled with other, "non-environmental" crisis tendencies and cannot be resolved in isolation from them. The political implications are conceptually simple if practically challenging: an ecopolitics capable of saving the planet must be both *anti-capitalist* and *trans-environmental*.

The historical reflections offered here deepen those propositions. What I first presented as an abstract 4-D logic, wherein capital is programmed to destabilize the natural conditions on which it depends, now appears as a concrete process, unfolding in space and time. Its trajectory looks like roughly this: a socio-ecological impasse originating in the core prompts a round of plunder in the periphery (including the periphery within the core), which targets the natural wealth of populations deprived of the political means of self-defense. In each case, too, the fix involves the conjure and appropriation of a new historical nature, previously dross but suddenly gold, a must-have world-commodity, conveniently viewed as unowned and there for the taking. What follows in each case, finally, are uncontrolled downstream effects, which spark new socioecological impasses, prompting further iterations of the cycle. And on and on.

Reiterated in each regime, this process unfolds expansively, on a world scale. Churning through sugar and silver, coal and guano, refined oil and chemical fertilizers, coltan and genetically modified seeds, it proceeds in stages, from conquest to colonization to neo-imperialism to financialization. The result is an evolving core/periphery geography, in which the boundary between those two co-constituted spaces shifts periodically, as does the boundary between economy and nature. The process that produces those shifts generates the distinctive spatiality of capitalist development.

That process also fashions capitalism's historical temporality. Each impasse is born from the collision of our three Natures, which operate on different timescales. In each episode, capital, in thrall to its fantasy of an eternally giving Nature II, able to self-replenish without end, reengineers Nature III to its own specifications, which dictate minimal outlays for eco-reproduction and maximal speed-up of turnover time; Nature I, meanwhile, proceeding on a time scale "of its own," registers the effects biophysically and "bites back." In time, the ensuing eco-damages converge with other, "non-environmental" harms, rooted in other, "non-environmental" contradictions of capitalist society. At that point, the regime in question enters its developmental crisis, leading to efforts to fashion a successor. Once installed, the latter reorganizes the nature/economy nexus in a way that dissolves the specific blockage but preserves the law of value, which commands maximum expansion of capital at maximum speed. Far from being overcome, then, capitalism's ecological contradiction is repeatedly displaced—in time as well as in space. The costs are off-loaded not "only" onto existing marginalized populations but also onto future generations. The lives of the latter, too, are discounted so that capital may live unencumbered and without end.

That last formulation suggests that the temporality of capitalism's ecological contradiction may not be "merely" developmental. Beneath the system's tendency to precipitate an unending string of regime-specific crises lies something deeper and more ominous: the prospect of an *epochal crisis*, rooted in centuries of escalating greenhouse gas emissions, whose volume now exceeds the earth's capacities for sequestration. The trans-regime progression of global warming portends a crisis of a different order. Implacably cumulating across the entire sequence of regimes and historical natures, climate change provides the perverse continuity of a ticking time bomb, which could bring the capitalist phase of human history—if not human history tout court—to an ignoble end.

To speak of an epochal crisis is *not*, however, to proclaim imminent breakdown. Nor does it rule out the advent of a new regime of accumulation that could provisionally manage or temporarily defer the current crisis. The truth is that we can't know for sure whether capitalism has any more tricks up its enormously inventive sleeve that could stave off global warming at least for a while; nor if so, for how long. Nor do we know whether the system's partisans could invent, sell, and implement those tricks quickly enough, given that they, and we, are in a race for time with Nature I. But this much is clear: anything more than a pro tem stopgap would require deep reordering of the economy/nature nexus, severely constraining, if not wholly abolishing, the prerogatives of capital.

Entangled Struggles

That conclusion vindicates my principal thesis: an eco-politics aimed at preventing catastrophe must be anti-capitalist and trans-environmental. If the rationale for the first of those adjectives is already clear, the justification for the second lies in the close connection, demonstrated here, between ecological depredation and other forms of dysfunction-cum-domination inherent in capitalist society. Consider, first, the internal links between natural despoliation and racial/imperial expropriation. Claims of terra nullius to the contrary, the chunks of nature that capital appropriates are virtually always the life conditions of some human group: their habitat and meaning-laden place of social interaction; their means of livelihood and material basis of social reproduction. Moreover, the human groups in capital's crosshairs are virtually always those that have been stripped of the power to defend themselves, and often those relegated to the wrong side of the global color line. This point was evidenced again and again throughout the sequence of regimes. It shows that ecological questions cannot be separated from questions of political power, on the one hand, nor from those of racial oppression, imperial domination, and indigenous dispossession and genocide, on the other hand.

A similar proposition holds for social reproduction, which is closely imbricated with natural reproduction. For most people, most of the time, ecosystemic damages add heavy stresses to the business of caregiving, social provision, and the tending of bodies and psyches—occasionally stretching social bonds to the breaking point. In most cases, too, the stresses bear down hardest on women, who shoulder primary responsibility for the well-being of families and communities. But there are exceptions that prove the rule. These arise when power asymmetries enable some groups to off-load the "externalities" onto others—as in the era of state-managed capitalism, when wealthy northern welfare states financed (more or less) generous social supports in the homeland by intensifying offshore extractivism. In that case, a political dynamic linking domestic social democracy to foreign domination enabled a racialized, gendered trade-off of social reproduction for ecodepredation—a bargain that capital's partisans later rescinded by designing a new, financialized regime that allowed them to have it both ways.

No wonder, then, that struggles over nature have been deeply entangled with struggles over labor, care, and political power in every phase of capitalist development. Nor that single-issue environmentalism is historically exceptional—and politically problematic. Recall the shifting forms and definitions of environmental struggle in the sequence of socioecological regimes. In the mercantile era, silver mining poisoned Peruvian lands and rivers, while land enclosures destroyed English woodlands, prompting considerable pushback in both cases. But participants in these struggles did not separate protection of nature or habitat from defense of livelihoods, political autonomy, or social reproduction of their communities. They fought, rather, for all those elements together—and for the forms of life in which they were integrated. When "nature defense" *did* appear as a freestanding cause, in the liberal-colonial era, it was among those whose livelihoods, communities, and political rights were *not* existentially threatened. Unencumbered by those other concerns, their stand-alone environmentalism was—necessarily—an environmentalism of the rich.[29]

As such, it contrasted starkly with contemporaneous social environmentalisms in the core and anti-colonial environmentalisms in the periphery, both of which targeted intertwined harms to nature and humans, anticipating present-day struggles for ecosocialism and environmental justice. But those movements were expunged from environmentalism's official history, which canonized the single-issue definition. The official definition broadened somewhat in the following era of state-managed capitalism, as wilderness protectionists were joined by activists urging direct deployment of capitalist state power against corporate polluters. What eco-successes this regime achieved were due to its use of that power, while its failures stemmed from the refusal to reckon seriously with trans-environmental entanglements—with the inherently trans-territorial character of emissions; with the force of homegrown environmental racism; with the power of capital to subvert regulation by lobbying, workarounds, and regulatory capture; and with the limitations intrinsic to a focus on eco-abuses as opposed to the normal, lawful workings of a fossil-fueled consumerist economy. Today, in the era of financialized capitalism, all those evasions are alive, well, and still wreaking havoc. Especially problematic, then and now, is the guiding premise that "the environment" can be adequately protected without disturbing the institutional framework and structural dynamics of capitalist society.

For a Trans-environmental, Anti-capitalist Eco-politics

Will these failures be repeated today? Will our chances to save the planet be squandered by our failure to build an ecopolitics that is trans-environmental and anti-capitalist? Many essential building blocks for such a politics already exist in one form or another. Environmental justice movements are already in principle trans-environmental, targeting entwinements of eco-damage with one or more axes of domination—usually gender, race, ethnicity and nationality—and some of them are explicitly anti-capitalist. Likewise, labor movements, Green New Dealers, and some eco-populists grasp (some of) the class prerequisites for fighting global warming—especially the need to link the transition to renewable energy to pro-working-class policies on incomes and jobs, and the need to strengthen the power of states against corporations. Finally, decolonial and indigenous movements plumb the entwinement of extractivism and imperialism. Along with degrowth currents, they press for a deep rethink of our relation to nature and ways of living. Each of these ecopolitical perspectives harbors some genuine insights.

Nevertheless, the current state of these movements is not (yet) adequate to the task at hand—whether viewed individually or as an ensemble. Insofar as environmental justice movements remain focused overwhelmingly on the disparate impact of eco-threats on subaltern populations, they fail to pay sufficient heed to the underlying structural dynamics of a social system that produces not only disparities in outcomes but a *general crisis* that threatens the well-being of all, not to mention the planet. Thus, their anti-capitalism is not yet sufficiently substantive, their trans-environmentalism not yet sufficiently deep.

Something similar is true of state-focused movements, especially (reactionary) eco-populists, but also (progressive) Green New Dealers and labor unions. Insofar as these actors privilege the frame of the national-territorial state and job creation through green infrastructure projects, they presume an insufficiently broad and variegated view of "the working class," which in reality includes not just construction workers, but also caregivers and service workers; not only those who work for a wage, but also those whose work is unpaid; not just those who work "in the homeland," but also those who work offshore; not only those who are exploited, but also those who are expropriated. Nor do state-focused currents adequately reckon with the position and power of that class's opposite number insofar as they retain the classic social democratic premise that the state can serve two masters—that is, that it can save the planet by taming capital and needn't abolish it. Thus, they too remain insufficiently anti-capitalist and trans-environmental—at least at present.

Finally, degrowth activists tend to muddy the political waters by conflating what *must* grow in capitalism—namely "value"—with what *should grow but can't* within capitalism —namely goods, relations, and activities that can satisfy the vast expanse of unmet human needs across the globe. A genuinely anti-capitalist ecopolitics must dismantle the hardwired imperative to grow the first, while treating the question of how sustainably to grow the second as a political matter, to be decided by democratic deliberation and social planning. Equally, orientations associated with degrowth, such as lifestyle environmentalism, on the one hand, and prefigurative experiments in commoning, on the other, tend to evade the necessity of confronting capitalist power.

Taken together, moreover, the genuine insights of these movements do not yet add up to a new ecopolitical common sense. Nor do they yet converge on a counterhegemonic project for eco-societal transformation that could, at least in principle, save the planet. Essential trans-environmental elements—labor rights, feminism, anti-racism, anti-imperialism, class consciousness, pro-democracy, anti-consumerism, anti-extractivism—are present, to be sure. But they are not yet integrated in a robust diagnosis of the structural-cum-historical roots of the present crisis. What is missing to date is a clear and convincing perspective that connects all of our present woes, ecological and otherwise, to one and the same social system—and through that to one another.

I have insisted here that that system has a name: capitalist society, conceived expansively to include all the necessary background conditions for a capitalist economy—nonhuman nature and public power, expropriation and social reproduction —all non-accidentally subject to cannibalization by capital, all now under the wrecking ball and reeling from it. To name that system, and conceive it broadly, is to supply another piece of the counterhegemonic puzzle we need to solve. This piece can help us to align the others, to disclose their likely tensions and potential synergies, to clarify where they have come from and where they might go together. Anti-capitalism is the piece that gives political direction and critical force to trans-environmentalism. If the latter opens ecopolitics to the larger world, the former trains its focus on the main enemy.

Anti-capitalism is thus what draws the line, necessary to every historical bloc, between "us" and "them." Unmasking carbon trading as the scam that it is, it pushes every potentially emancipatory current of ecopolitics to publicly disaffiliate from "green capitalism." It pushes each current, too, to pay heed to its own Achilles' heel—its inclination to avoid confronting capital—whether by pursuing (illusory) de-linking, (lopsided) class compromise, or (tragic) parity in extreme vulnerability. By insisting on their common enemy, moreover, the anti-capitalism piece of the puzzle indicates a path that partisans of degrowth, environmental justice, and a Green New Deal can travel together, even if they can't now envision, let alone agree on, its precise destination.

It remains to be seen, of course, whether any destination will actually be reached—or whether the earth will continue to heat to the boiling point. But our best hope for avoiding the latter fate is, once again, to build a counterhegemonic bloc that is trans-environmental and anti-capitalist. Where exactly such a bloc should aim to lead us remains obscure as well. But if I had to give the goal a name, I'd opt for "ecosocialism."

To clarify prospects for such a project, I turn in the following chapter to the political strand of cannibal capitalism's current crisis.

5

Butchering Democracy: Why Political Crisis Is Capital's Red Meat

We are currently facing a crisis of democracy. That much is beyond dispute. What is less well understood, however, is that this crisis is not freestanding, and its sources do not lie exclusively in the political realm. Contrary to bien-pensant common sense, it cannot be overcome by restoring civility, cultivating bipartisanship, opposing tribalism, or defending truth-oriented, fact-based discourse. Nor, contra recent democratic theory, can this crisis be resolved by reforming the political realm—not, that is, by strengthening "the democratic ethos," reactivating "the constituent power," unleashing the force of "agonism," or fostering "democratic iterations."[1] All these proposals fall prey to an error I call "politicism." By analogy with economism, politicist thinking overlooks the causal force of extra-political society. Treating the political order as self-determining, it fails to problematize the larger societal matrix that generates its deformations.

Make no mistake: democracy's present crisis is firmly anchored in a societal matrix. Like the impasses analyzed in previous chapters, it represents one strand of a broader crisis complex and cannot be understood in isolation from that. Neither freestanding nor merely sectoral, today's democratic ills form the specifically political strand of the general crisis that is engulfing our societal order in its entirety. Their underlying bases lie in the sinews of that order—in the latter's institutional structures and constitutive dynamics. Bound up with processes that transcend the political, democratic crisis can only be grasped by a critical perspective on the social totality.

What exactly is this social totality? Many astute observers identify it with neoliberalism—and not without reason. It is true, as Colin Crouch maintains, that democratic governments are now outgunned, if not wholly captured, by oligopolistic corporations with a global reach, lately liberated from public control.[2] It is also true, as Wolfgang Streeck contends, that democracy's decline in the Global North coincides with a coordinated tax revolt of corporate capital and the installation of global financial markets as the new sovereigns that elected governments must obey.[3] Nor can one dispute Wendy Brown's claim that democratic power is being hollowed out from within by neoliberal political rationalities that valorize efficiency and choice and by modes of subjectivation that enjoin "self-responsibilization" and maximization of one's "human capital."[4] Finally, Stephen Gill is right to insist that democratic action is being preempted by a "new constitutionalism" that locks in neoliberal macroeconomic policy transnationally, through treaties such as the Agreement on Trade-Related Aspects of Intellectual Property (TRIPS) and the North American Free Trade Agreement (NAFTA), which enshrine free trade strictures as political trumps and foreclose robust social and environmental legislation in the public interest.[5] Whether taken individually or read together, these accounts convey the entirely plausible idea that what threatens our democracy is neoliberalism.

Nevertheless, the problem runs deeper. Neoliberalism is, after all, a form of capitalism, and today's democratic crisis is by no means capitalism's first. Nor is it likely, if capitalism perdures, to be the last. On the contrary, *every* major phase of capitalist development has given rise to, and been transformed by, political turmoil. Mercantile capitalism was periodically roiled—and eventually destroyed—by a slew of peripheral slave revolts and metropolitan democratic revolutions. Its laissez-faire successor racked up a solid century and a half of political turbulence, including multiple socialist revolutions and fascist putsches, two world wars and countless anti-colonial uprisings, before giving way in the inter- and postwar era to state-managed capitalism. The latter regime was itself no stranger to political crisis, having weathered a massive wave of anti-colonial rebellions, a global New Left uprising, a protracted Cold War, and a nuclear arms race before succumbing to neoliberal subversion, which ushered in the current regime of globalizing, financialized capitalism.

This history casts the present democratic crisis in a different light. Neoliberalism's political travails, however acute, represent the latest chapter of a longer story, which concerns the political vicissitudes of capitalism as such. Not just neoliberalism, but *capitalism*, is prone to political crisis and inimical to democracy.

That is the guiding premise of the present chapter. Here, I treat democracy's present woes as part of the general crisis of contemporary financialized capitalism. But I also follow the practice of previous chapters in arguing a stronger thesis: not just this form, but *every* form of capitalism harbors a contradiction that inclines it to political crisis. Like those discussed earlier in this book, this "political" contradiction, as I shall call it, is inscribed in the system's DNA. Far from representing an anomaly, then, the democratic crisis we experience today is the form this contradiction assumes in capitalism's present, financialized phase.

The Political Contradiction of Capitalism "As Such"

My argument relies on the enlarged understanding of capitalism I elaborated in chapter 1. As I noted there, many left-wing thinkers understand capitalism too narrowly, as an economic system simpliciter. Focused on contradictions internal to the economy, they equate capitalist crisis with economic dysfunctions, such as depressions, bankruptcy chains, and market crashes. The effect is to preclude a full accounting of capitalism's crisis tendencies, omitting its non-economic contradictions and forms of crisis. What are excluded, above all, are crises grounded in *inter-realm contradictions*—contradictions that arise when capitalism's economic imperatives collide with the reproduction imperatives of the non-economic realms whose health is essential to ongoing accumulation, not to mention to human well-being.

An example, explored in chapter 3, is the social reproductive contradiction of capitalist society. Marxists have rightly located the secret of accumulation in the "hidden abode" of commodity production, where capital exploits wage labor. But they have not always fully appreciated that this process rests on the even more hidden abode of unwaged carework, often performed by women, which forms and replenishes the human subjects who constitute "labor." Deeply dependent on such social-reproductive activities, capital nonetheless accords them no (monetized) value, treats them as free and infinitely available, and makes little or no effort to sustain them. Left to itself, therefore, and given its relentless drive to limitless accumulation, it is always in danger of destabilizing the very processes of social reproduction on which it depends.

Another example, elaborated in chapter 4, is capitalism's ecological contradiction. On the one hand, the accumulation of capital relies on nature—both as a "tap," which supplies material and energic inputs to commodity production, and as a "sink" for absorbing the latter's waste. On the other hand, capital disavows the ecological costs it generates, effectively assuming that nature can replenish itself autonomously and without end. In this case, too, the serpent tends to eat its own tail, cannibalizing the natural conditions on which it relies. In both cases, an inter-realm contradiction grounds a proclivity to a type of capitalist crisis that transcends the economic: social reproductive crisis, in one case, and ecological crisis, in the other.

I now propose to apply the same logic to democracy's present travails—and thereby to escape the trap of politicism. Seen this way, our current political impasses no longer appear as free-standing. They are grounded, rather, in another inter-realm contradiction—in this case between the imperatives of capital accumulation and the maintenance of the public powers on which accumulation also relies. The nub of the trouble can be stated like this: legitimate, efficacious public power is a condition of possibility for sustained capital accumulation; yet capital's drive to endless accumulation tends over time to destabilize the very public powers on which it depends. This contradiction lies, I will argue here, at the root of our present democratic crisis. But as I'll also argue, the latter is inextricably entwined with the system's other impasses and cannot be resolved on its own.

Public Powers

Let us pursue this hypothesis by noting, first, that capital relies on public powers to establish and enforce its constitutive norms. Accumulation is inconceivable, after all, in the absence of a legal framework underpinning private enterprise and market exchange. It depends crucially on public powers to guarantee property rights, enforce contracts, and adjudicate disputes; to suppress rebellions, maintain order, and manage dissent; to sustain the monetary regimes that constitute capital's lifeblood; to undertake efforts to forestall or manage crises; and to codify and enforce both official status hierarchies, such as those that distinguish citizens from "aliens," and also unofficial ones, such as those that distinguish free exploitable workers, who are entitled to sell their labor power, from dependent, expropriable "others," whose assets and persons can simply be seized.

Historically, the public powers in question have mostly been lodged in territorial states, including those that operated as colonial powers. It was the legal systems of such states that established seemingly depoliticized arenas within which private actors could pursue their "economic" interests, free from "political" interference. Likewise, it was territorial states that mobilized "legitimate force" to put down resistance to the expropriations through which capitalist property relations were originated and sustained. Then, too, it was national states that conferred subjective rights upon some and denied them to others. It was such states, finally, that nationalized and underwrote money. Having thus constituted the capitalist economy, these political powers took subsequent steps to fortify capital's ability to accumulate profits and face down challenges. They built and maintained infrastructure, compensated for "market failures," steered economic development, bolstered social reproduction, mitigated economic crises, and managed the associated political fallout.

But that is not all. A capitalist economy also has political conditions of possibility at the geopolitical level. At issue here is the organization of the broader space in which territorial states are embedded. This is a space in which capital would seem to move quite easily, given its inherent expansionist thrust and its deep-seated drive to siphon wealth from peripheral regions to its core. But its ability to operate across borders, to expand through international trade, and to profit from the predation of subjugated peoples depends not only on national-imperial military might, but also on transnational political arrangements: on international law, brokered agreements among the Great Powers, and supranational regimes that partially pacify (in a capital-friendly way) a global space that is sometimes imagined as a state of nature. Throughout its history, capitalism's economy has depended on the military and organizational capacities of a succession of global hegemons, which have sought to foster accumulation on a progressively expanding scale within the framework of a multistate political system.[6]

At both levels, then, the state-territorial and the geopolitical, the capitalist economy is deeply indebted to political powers external to it. These "non-economic" powers are indispensable to all the major streams of accumulation: to the exploitation of (doubly) free labor and the production and exchange of commodities; to the expropriation of racialized subject peoples and the siphoning of wealth from periphery to core; to the organization of finance, space, and knowledge; and to the accrual of interest and rent. In no way marginal adjuncts, political forces (like social reproduction and nonhuman nature) are constitutive elements of capitalist society. Essential to its functioning, public power is part and parcel of the institutionalized societal order that is capitalism.

Nevertheless, the maintenance of political power stands in tense relation with the imperative of capital accumulation. The reason lies in capitalism's distinctive institutional topography, which separates "the economic" from "the political." In this respect, capitalist societies differ from earlier forms, in which those instances were effectively fused—as, for example, in feudal society, where control over labor, land, and military force was vested in the single institution of lordship and vassalage. In capitalist society, by contrast, economic power and political power are split apart; each is assigned its own sphere, endowed with its own distinctive medium and modus operandi.[7] The power to organize production is privatized and devolved to capital, which is supposed to deploy only the "natural," "nonpolitical" sanctions of hunger and need. The task of governing "non-economic" orders, including those that supply the external conditions for accumulation, falls to the public power, which alone may utilize the "political" media of law and "legitimate" state violence. In capitalism, therefore, the economic is nonpolitical, and the political is non-economic.

Constitutive of capitalism as an institutionalized societal order, this separation severely limits the scope of the political within that order. Devolving vast aspects of social life to the rule of "the market" (in reality, to large corporations), it declares them off limits to democratic decision making, collective action, and public control. The arrangement deprives us of the ability to decide collectively what and how much we want to produce, on what energic basis and through what kinds of social relations. It deprives us, too, of the capacity to determine how we want to use the social surplus we collectively produce; how we want to relate to nature and to future generations; how we want to organize the work of social reproduction and its relation to that of production. By virtue of its inherent structure, then, capitalism is fundamentally anti-democratic. Even in the best-case scenario, democracy in a capitalist society must perforce be limited and weak.

But capitalist society is typically not at its best, and whatever democracy it manages to accommodate must also be shaky and insecure. The trouble is that capital, by its very nature, tries to have it both ways. On the one hand, it freeloads off of public power, availing itself of the legal regimes, repressive forces, infrastructures, and regulatory agencies that are indispensable to accumulation. At the same time, the thirst for profit periodically tempts some fractions of the capitalist class to rebel against public power, to bad-mouth it as inferior to markets, and to scheme to weaken it. In such cases, when short-term interests trump long-term survival, capital once again threatens to destroy the very political conditions of its own possibility.

Here, then, is a political contradiction lodged deep in the institutional structure of capitalist society. Like the other contradictions I have discussed, this one, too, grounds a crisis tendency, one that is not located "inside" the economy, but rather at the border that simultaneously separates and connects economy and polity in capitalist society. Inherent in capitalism as such, this inter-realm contradiction inclines *every* form of capitalist society to political crisis.

Political Crises in Capitalism's History

So far, I have been elaborating the structure of this political crisis tendency for capitalism as such. However, capitalist society does not exist "as such," but only in historically specific forms or regimes of accumulation. And far from being given once and for all, capitalism's constitutive division between "the economic" and "the political" is subject to contestation and to change. Especially in periods of crisis, social actors struggle over the boundaries delimiting economy from polity—and sometimes succeed in redrawing them. In the twentieth century, for example, sharpening class conflict forced states to take on new responsibilities for promoting employment and economic growth. In the lead-up to the twenty-first, by contrast, partisans of the "free market" altered the international rules of the road in ways that strongly incentivized states to abandon such efforts. The result, in both cases, was to revise previously established boundaries between economy and polity. That division has mutated several times in the course of capitalism's history, as have the public powers that made accumulation possible at every stage.

Products of what, in chapter 1, I called "boundary struggles," such shifts mark epochal transformations of capitalist society. If we adopt a perspective that foregrounds them, we can distinguish political analogues of the four historical regimes of accumulation that I identified in previous chapters: an early modern regime of mercantile capitalism, a nineteenth-century regime of liberal-colonial capitalism, a mid-twentieth-century regime of state-managed monopoly capitalism, and the current regime of globalizing financialized capitalism. In each case, the political conditions for the capitalist economy assumed a different institutional form at both the state-territorial and geopolitical levels. In each case, too, the political contradiction of capitalist society assumed a different guise and found expression in a different set of crisis phenomena. In each regime, finally, capitalism's political contradiction incited different forms of social struggle.

Consider, first, capitalism's initial, mercantile phase, which held sway for a couple hundred years, roughly from the sixteenth to the eighteenth centuries. In this phase, capitalism's economy was only partially separated from the state. Neither land nor labor was a true commodity, and moral-economic norms still governed most everyday interactions, even in the towns and cities of the European heartland. Absolutist rulers used their powers to regulate commerce within their territories, even as they profited from external plunder (effected through military force) and from long-distance trade (organized capitalistically under first Genovese and then Dutch hegemony) through an expanding world market in slaves, precious metals, and luxury commodities. The result was an internal/external division: commercial regulation inside the national territory, "the law of value" outside it.

Although that division held for a while, it could not in the end be sustained. The tensions within this order intensified as the value logic that operated internationally began to penetrate the domestic space of European states, altering the social relations among landowners and their dependents and fostering new professional and business milieus in urban centers, which became seedbeds of liberal, even revolutionary, thinking. Equally corrosive—and consequential—was the rising indebtedness of rulers. In desperate need of revenue, some of them were forced to convene proto-parliamentary bodies that they could not, in the end, control. And that led in several cases to revolution.

Thanks to this combination of economic corrosion and political turmoil, mercantile capitalism was supplanted in the nineteenth century by a new regime, often called "liberal" or "laissez-faire" capitalism—although, as we shall see, those terms are highly misleading. In this phase, the economy/polity nexus was reconfigured. Leading European capitalist states no longer used public power directly to regulate internal commerce. Rather, they constructed "economies," in which production and exchange appeared to operate autonomously, free from overt political control, through the "purely economic" mechanism of supply and demand. What underlay that construction was a new legal order, which enshrined the supremacy of contract, private property, price-setting markets, and the associated subjective rights of "free individuals," viewed as utility-maximizing, arm's-length transactors. The effect was to institutionalize, at the national level, a seemingly sharp division between the public power of states, on the one hand, and the private power of capital, on the other.

But, of course, states were all the while using repressive power to sanctify the land expropriations that transformed rural populations into doubly free proletarians. In this way, they established the class preconditions for the large-scale exploitation of wage labor, which, when combined with fossilized energy, powered a massive takeoff of industrial manufacturing—and with it, intense class conflict. In some metropolitan states, militant labor movements and their allies were able to force a class compromise. Majority-ethnicity workingmen won the vote and political citizenship, while effectively conceding capital's right to rule the workplace and exploit them in it. In the periphery, by contrast, no such compromises were forthcoming. Dropping every pretense of political abstinence, European colonial powers marshaled military might to crush anti-imperial rebellions. Ensuring that wholesale looting of subjugated populations could continue, they consolidated colonial rule on the basis of free trade imperialism under British hegemony—all of which raises doubts about the expression "laissez-faire capitalism" and leads me to speak instead of "liberal-colonial capitalism."

Virtually from the start, moreover, this regime was wracked by instability, both economic and political. In the democratizing countries of the core, political equality stood in a tense relation with socioeconomic inequality; and the political rights extended there sat uneasily in the minds of some with the brutal subjection ongoing in the periphery. Equally corrosive was the contradiction, diagnosed by the political thinker Hannah Arendt, between the unlimited, trans-territorializing thrust of liberal-colonial capitalism's economic logic and the limited, territorially bounded character of its democratic polities.[8] No wonder, then, that as Karl Polanyi stressed in *The Great Transformation*, this economy/polity configuration proved chronically crisis ridden. On the economic side, "liberal" capitalism was roiled by periodic depressions, crashes, and panics; on the political side, it generated intense class conflicts, boundary struggles, and revolutions—all fueling and fueled by international financial chaos, anti-colonial rebellions, and inter-imperialist wars.[9] By the twentieth century, the multiple contradictions of this form of capitalism had metastasized into a protracted general crisis, which was finally resolved only in the aftermath of the Second World War with the installation of a new regime.

In this new, state-managed capitalist regime, the states of the core began to use public power more proactively within their own territories to forestall or mitigate crisis. Empowered by the Bretton Woods system of capital controls, which had been established in 1944 under US hegemony, they invested in infrastructure, assumed some costs of social reproduction, promoted (something approaching) full employment and working-class consumerism, accepted labor unions as partners in trilateral corporatist bargaining, actively steered economic development, compensated for "market failures," and generally disciplined capital for its own good. Aimed in part at securing the conditions for sustained private capital accumulation, these measures broadened the purview of politics while simultaneously taming it: they incorporated potentially revolutionary strata by augmenting the worth of their citizenship and giving them a stake in the system. The effect was to stabilize matters for several decades, but at a cost. Arrangements that delivered "social citizenship" to majority-ethnicity industrial workers in the capitalist core rested on some not-so-nice background conditions: on women's dependency through the family wage, on racial and ethnic exclusions, and on ongoing imperial expropriation in what was then called the Third World. The latter proceeded, by old means and new, even after decolonization, severely limiting the capacities of newly independent states to stabilize their societies, steer development, and protect their populations from market-mediated predation. The effect was to plant some ticking political time bombs, whose detonation would eventually converge with other processes to bring down this regime.

In the end, state-managed capitalism, too, ran up against its own contradictions, both economic and political. Rising wages and the generalization of productivity gains combined to lower profit rates in manufacturing in the core, prompting new efforts on the part of capital to unshackle market forces from political regulation. Meanwhile, a global New Left erupted to challenge the oppressions, exclusions, and predations on which the whole edifice rested. What followed was a protracted period of crisis, at times acute, at times slow boiling, during which the state-managed capitalist settlement was stealthily supplanted by the present regime of financialized capitalism—to which I now turn.

A Double Whammy

Financialized capitalism has remade the economy/polity relation yet again. In this regime, central banks and global financial institutions have replaced states as the arbiters of an increasingly globalized economy. It is they, not states, who now make many of the most consequential rules that govern the central relations of capitalist society: between labor and capital, citizens and states, core and periphery, and—crucial for all of the above—between debtors and creditors. These last relations are central to financialized capitalism and permeate all of the others. It is largely through debt that capital now cannibalizes labor, disciplines states, transfers value from periphery to core, and sucks wealth from society and nature. As debt flows through states, regions, communities, households, and firms, the result is a dramatic shift in the relation of economy to polity.

The previous regime had empowered states to subordinate the short-term interests of private firms to the long-term objective of sustained accumulation. By contrast, this one authorizes finance capital to discipline states and publics in the immediate interests of private investors. The effect is a double whammy. On the one hand, the state institutions that were previously (somewhat) responsive to citizens are increasingly incapable of solving the latter's problems or meeting their needs. On the other hand, the central banks and global financial institutions that have hobbled state capacities are "politically independent": unaccountable to publics and free to act on behalf of investors and creditors. Meanwhile, the scale of pressing problems, such as global warming, exceeds the reach and heft of public powers. The latter are, in any case, overmatched by transnational corporations and global financial flows, which elude control by political agencies tethered to bounded territories. The general result is the growing incapacity of public powers to rein in private powers. Hence the association of financialized capitalism with such neologisms as "de-democratization" and "post-democracy."

The shift to a regime centered on accumulation through debt arose through a major restructuring of the international order. Central here were the dismantling of the Bretton Woods framework of capital controls, fixed exchange rates, and convertibility to gold, on the one hand, and the repurposing of the World Bank and the International Monetary Fund as agents of economic liberalization, on the other hand—both moves pushed by the United States and serving to prolong its hegemony. There soon followed, from the 1980s onward, the US-led assault on the developmental state, first via "the Washington Consensus" and then via "structural adjustment." As liberalization was imposed at the gunpoint of debt throughout much of the Global South, indebted states scrambled for hard currency by opening export processing zones and by promoting labor emigration for the sake of remittances. Meanwhile, the relocation of manufacturing to the semi-periphery empowered capital in two respects: first, by instituting a race to the bottom in the South, and second, by decimating powerful trade unions in the capitalist core, thereby weakening political support for social democracy. Meanwhile, the abolition of capital controls and the creation of the euro deprived nearly all states of control over their currencies, putting them at the mercy of bond markets and ratings agencies, and disabling a critical tool of crisis management.[10] The states of the core were thrust into a position long familiar to those of the periphery: subjection to global economic forces they could not possibly hope to control.

One response was a policy shift, memorably named by Colin Crouch, from public to privatized Keynesianism.[11] Whereas the first had utilized tax and spend to prime the pump of consumer demand, the second encouraged consumer debt to promote continued high levels of consumer spending under otherwise-unfavorable conditions of falling real wages, rising precarity, and declining corporate tax revenues. That shift, ramped up to new heights of dizziness by "securitization," brought us the subprime crisis that triggered the near meltdown of global finance in 2007–8. The latter's outcome could not have been more perverse. Far from prompting deep restructuring of the economy/polity nexus, the response of the powers-that-be solidified the hold of private creditors over public power. Having orchestrated sovereign debt crises, central banks and global financial institutions compelled states under assault by bond markets to institute "austerity," which meant serving up their citizens on a platter for cannibalization by international lenders. The European Union, once considered the avatar of "postnational democracy," rushed to do the bidding of the bankers and investors, forfeiting its claim to democratic legitimacy in the eyes of many.

Generally, financialized capitalism is the era of "governance without government"—which is to say, that of domination without the fig leaf of consent. In this regime, it is not states but transnational governance structures such as the European Union, World Trade Organization, NAFTA, and TRIPS that make the lion's share of the coercively enforceable rules that now govern vast swaths of social interaction throughout the world. Accountable to no one and acting overwhelmingly in the interest of capital, these bodies are "constitutionalizing" neoliberal notions of "free trade" and "intellectual property," hard-wiring them into the global regime, and preempting democratic labor and environmental legislation in advance. Through a variety of means, finally, this regime has promoted the capture of public power by private (corporate) power, while also colonizing the former internally, modeling its modus operandi on that of private firms.

The overall effect has been to hollow out public power at every level. Political agendas are everywhere narrowed, both by external fiat (the demands of "the markets," "the new constitutionalism") and by internal co-optation (corporate capture, privatization, the spread of neoliberal political rationality). Matters once considered to be squarely within the purview of democratic political action are now declared off limits and devolved to "the markets"—that is, to the benefit of finance and corporate capital. And woe unto those who object. In the current regime, capital's enablers brazenly target any public powers or political forces that might challenge the new dispensation, whether by nullifying elections and referenda that reject austerity, as in Greece in 2015, or by preventing the candidacies of popular figures who appear likely to choose that path, as in Brazil in 2017–18. Throughout this era, meanwhile, leading capitalist interests (Big Fruit, Big Pharma, Big Energy, Big Arms, Big Data) have continued their long-standing practice of promoting authoritarianism and repression, imperialism and war throughout the world. We owe the current refugee crisis in large part to them, as well as to the state actors to whom they are tied.

In general, then, the present regime of accumulation has spawned a crisis of democratic governance. But far from being freestanding, this crisis is grounded in the contradictory, self-destabilizing dynamics of capitalist society. What some call our "democratic deficit" is actually the historically specific form that capitalism's inherent political contradiction assumes in its present phase—one where runaway financialization inundates the political realm, diminishing its powers to the point that it cannot solve pressing problems, including those, such as global heating, that endanger long-term prospects for accumulation, not to mention life on planet Earth. In this phase of capitalism, as in every other, democratic crisis is not merely sectoral, but an aspect of a larger crisis complex that also includes other aspects —ecological, social-reproductive, and economic. Inextricably entwined with those others, our present democratic crisis is an integral strand of the general crisis of financialized capitalism. It cannot be resolved short of resolving the general crisis—hence, without transforming that societal order root and branch.

A Momentous Historical Crossroads

Nevertheless, there is more to be said about the current democratic crisis. To this point, I have considered it chiefly from a structural perspective, as the non-accidental unfolding of contradictions inherent in financialized capitalism. That perspective is indispensable, as I have argued here and in the preceding chapters. But it does not suffice to clarify the full extent of the present crisis, which, like every general crisis, also includes a hegemonic dimension.

A crisis, after all, is not simply a logjam in the societal mechanism. Neither an obstruction in the circuits of accumulation nor a blockage in the system of governance merits the label "crisis" in the true sense. That sense includes not only systemic impasses but also the responses to them of social actors. Contrary to impoverished "systems-theoretic" understandings, nothing fully counts as a crisis until it is experienced as such. What looks like a crisis to an outside observer does not become historically generative until participants in the society see it *as* a crisis—until, for example, they intuit that the pressing problems they experience arise not despite but precisely *because of* the established order and cannot be solved within it. Only then, when a critical mass resolves that the order can and must be transformed by collective action, does an objective impasse gain a subjective voice. Then, and only then, can we speak of crisis in the larger sense of a momentous historical crossroads that demands a decision.[12]

That is exactly our situation today. No longer "merely" objective, the political dysfunctions of financialized capitalism have found a subjective correlative. What observers might earlier have deemed a crisis-in-itself has become a crisis-for-itself, as masses of people throughout the world have defected from politics as usual. The most dramatic break occurred in 2016, when voters in two major citadels of global finance rebuked the political architects of neoliberalism by delivering victories to Brexit and Donald Trump. But the process was already underway, both there and elsewhere, as populations abandoned ruling centrist parties that promoted financialization for populist upstarts who claimed to oppose it. In many regions, right-wing populists successfully courted majority-ethnic working-class voters by promising to "take back" their countries from global capital, "invading" immigrants, and racial or religious minorities. Their left-wing counterparts, although less successful electorally (except in Latin America and southern Europe), made strong showings in civil society, militating for "the 99 percent" or "working families," defined inclusively, and against a system "rigged" to favor "the billionaire class."

Certainly, these political formations differ importantly among themselves, and their respective fortunes have waxed and waned in subsequent years. But taken together, and viewed overall, their emergence signaled a major shift in the political winds. Having pierced the veil of neoliberal common sense and deflated its romance of the market, the populist wave emboldened many to think outside the box. Absent the "certainty" that social coordination was best achieved via global free market competition among private firms, the scope for political invention broadened, and heretofore unthinkable alternatives became conceivable. The result is a new phase in the gestation of capitalist crisis. A "mere" conglomeration of system impasses is now a full-blown crisis of hegemony.[13]

At the center of this hegemonic crisis is an open dispute over the current boundary between economy and polity. No longer self-evident, the idea that public planning is vastly inferior to competitive markets now meets serious pushback. Responding to climate change and the COVID-19 pandemic, as well as to ballooning class inequality and rampant racial injustice, newly energized social democrats join populists and democratic socialists in seeking to rehabilitate public power. Some, assuming the national frame, champion bold government action to protect citizens from the devastating effects of financialization—economic, ecological, social, and political. Others—alter-globalization and environmental-justice activists —envision new public powers, global or transnational in scope, with the heft and reach to rein in investors and overcome transborder threats to planetary well-being. There are disagreements, to be sure, as to the depth of restructuring required. Social democrats and populists believe that governments can guarantee jobs and incomes, public health, and a habitable planet without disturbing capitalism's underlying property relations and accumulation dynamic. Socialists and radical ecologists disagree. That such matters are debated publicly is proof enough that neoliberal common sense has crumbled. It testifies, too, to something more: there now exists a substantial, if internally fractured, constituency that aims to redraw the boundary between economy and polity so as to strengthen the ability of the second to govern the first.

That proposition got a boost from the COVID-19 pandemic. Notwithstanding upsurges of anti-mask, anti-vax libertarianism and economy-über-alles zealotry, the coronavirus served as a textbook vindication of public power: of the urgent need for public action to maintain infrastructures and assure supply chains; to flatten the curve of infections by mandating mask wearing, social distancing, and sheltering in place; to slow transmission by testing, tracking, and isolating those infected; to develop, fund, test, approve, and distribute vaccines and therapeutics; to protect frontline workers and at-risk populations; to support incomes and maintain living standards; to organize caregiving and schooling—all in ways that ensured an equitable distribution of burdens and benefits. It turned out that none of these vital needs could be met by the private sector. Extreme national disparities in outcomes proved the point. When it came to reducing infection rates and saving lives, countries whose political cultures valorized public power and authorized its broad, proactive deployment far outperformed those that disparaged it and restricted its use. If we lived in a rational world, neoliberalism would be a receding memory.[14]

But we live, rather, in a capitalist world, which is by definition rife with irrationality. Thus, we cannot assume that the present crisis will be resolved quickly or without a fight. On the contrary, the representatives of financial and corporate capital maintain a solid grip on the institutional levers of power at the transnational and global levels, where neoliberal rules of the road remain in force and still block popular efforts to plot a new course. At the national level, moreover, capital's proxies still maneuver, with much success, to hold or regain political power, notwithstanding overt opposition. They consolidate support even—or especially—where their populist challengers come to power and disappoint.

That last scenario came to the pass in the United States, where Donald Trump, on assuming the presidency in 2016, ditched the pro–working class policies on which he had campaigned in favor of pro-corporate alternatives. Notwithstanding herculean efforts to distract by massively ramped-up scapegoating, enough Trump supporters defected in a handful of crucial swing states to seal his defeat in 2020 by, of all people, an Obama alumnus who pledged to restore the progressive-neoliberal status quo ante—despite the fact that it was that regime that created the conditions that brought us Trumpism in the first place and that will continue to feed it to the last.[15] It must be acknowledged, however, that left-wing populist governments disappointed as well. The latter did not lack for internal failings, to be sure; but their derailments involved a hefty share of external forces: witness Syriza in Greece, brought to its knees by an EU "Troika" intent on demonstrating that no sincere effort to prioritize the needs of the 99 percent over those of investors would be allowed to stand.

In any case, there is something hollow about the Trumps, Bolsonaros, Modis, Erdogans, et al. Reminiscent of "The Wizard of Oz," they are like showmen who preen and strut in front of the curtain, while the real power hides behind it. The real power is, of course, capital: the mega-corporations, large investors, banks, and financial institutions whose unquenchable thirst for profit condemns billions of people across the globe to stunted and shortened lives. What's more, the showmen have no solutions to their supporters' problems; they're in bed with the very forces that created those problems. All they can do is distract with stunts and spectacles. As the impasses worsen and solutions fail to materialize, these front men are driven to up the ante with ever more outlandish lies and vicious scapegoating. That dynamic is bound to escalate until someone pulls back the curtain and exposes the sham.

And that is precisely what the mainstream progressive opposition has failed to do. Far from unmasking the powers behind the curtain, dominant currents of "the resistance" have long been entangled with them. That's the case for the liberal-meritocratic wings of such popular social movements as feminism, anti-racism, LGBTQ+ rights, and environmentalism. Operating under liberal hegemony, they have functioned for many years as junior partners in a progressive-neoliberal bloc that also included "forward thinking" sectors of global capital (IT, finance, media, entertainment). Thus, progressives, too, have served as front men, albeit in a different way—by casting a veneer of emancipatory charisma over the predatory political economy of neoliberalism.

The result, there can be no doubt, was far from emancipatory. It's not "just" that this unholy alliance ravaged the life conditions of the vast majority and thereby created the soil that nourished the Right. In addition, it associated feminism, anti-racism, etc., with neoliberalism, ensuring that when the dam finally broke, and masses of people rejected the latter, many of them would also reject the former. And that is why the principal beneficiary, at least so far, has been reactionary rightwing populism. It's also why we are now trapped in a political impasse, caught up in a sham diversionary battle between two sets of rival front men, one regressive, the other progressive, while the powers behind the curtain laugh all the way to the bank.

Where does this leave us today? Absent some new realignment, we face an unsettled terrain with no broadly legitimate hegemonic ruling bloc—nor any clear and credible counterhegemonic challenger. In this situation, the most likely near-term scenario is a series of pendulum swings, with governments oscillating back and forth between the frankly neoliberal (progressive or regressive, diversity-friendly or exclusionary, liberal-democratic or proto-fascist) and the professedly anti-neoliberal (left- or right-populist or social-democratic or communitarian), the precise mix to be determined in every case by national specificities.

Such political oscillations mark the present as an interregnum: a time when, in the words of Antonio Gramsci, "the old is dying and the new cannot be born." The duration of this interregnum is anyone's guess, as is the likelihood of its devolution into full-bore authoritarianism, major war, or catastrophic meltdown—as opposed to "mere" slow unraveling. One way or another, the system's impasses will continue to grind away at our ways of life, until such time as a credible counterhegemonic bloc can be assembled. Until then, we will live (and die) amid the vast array of "morbid symptoms" that mark the death throes of financialized capitalism, and the general crisis it has wrought.

Whatever happens, this much is clear: crises like this one do not come along every day. Historically rare, they represent hinge points in capitalism's history, decision moments when the shape of social life is up for grabs. At such times, the burning question is: Who will succeed in constructing a viable counterhegemony, and on what basis? Who, in other words, will guide the process of social transformation, in whose interest, and to what end? As we saw, the process whereby general crisis leads to societal reorganization has played out several times in modern history—largely to capital's benefit. Through this process, capitalism has reinvented itself again and again. Seeking to restore profitability and tame opposition, its champions have redrawn the economy/polity division, reconfiguring both of those "realms," as well as their relation to one another and to social reproduction, nonhuman nature, and race and empire. In so doing, they have reorganized not only the mode of political domination, but also the established forms of exploitation and expropriation—hence, class domination and status hierarchy, as well as political subjection. Reinventing those fault lines anew, they have often managed to channel rebellious energies into new hegemonic projects that overwhelmingly benefit capital.

Will this process be repeated today?

The struggle to resolve the present democratic crisis, like that crisis itself, cannot be limited to one sector of society, or one strand of the overall crisis. Far from concerning political institutions alone, it poses the most fundamental and general questions of social organization: Where will we draw the line delimiting economy from polity, society from nature, production from reproduction? How will we allocate our time among work and leisure, family life, politics, and civil society? How will we use the social surplus we collectively produce? And who exactly will decide these matters? Will the profit-makers manage to turn capitalism's contradictions into new opportunities for the accumulation of private wealth? Will they co-opt important strands of rebellion, even as they reorganize social domination? Or will a mass revolt against capital finally be, as Walter Benjamin wrote, "the act by which the human race travelling in [this runaway] train applies the emergency brake"?[16]

The answer depends in part on how we understand the present crisis. If we stick to familiar politicist interpretations, we will construe democracy's travails as a freestanding species of political trouble. We will moralize about the need for civility, bipartisanship, and respect for the truth while ignoring the deep-structural sources of the trouble. Sailing high-mindedly above the concerns of the benighted "deplorables," we will discount the claims of those critical masses across the globe that are rejecting neoliberalism and demanding fundamental change. Failing to recognize their legitimate grievances (however wrongly interpreted and misdirected), we will render ourselves irrelevant in the present struggle to build a counter-hegemony. The alternative, which I have sketched here, is to view democracy's current travails as expressing deep-seated contradictions built into the institutional structure of financialized capitalism—that is, as one component of the roiling general crisis of our societal order. Apart from its substantive strengths, that interpretation has the further merit of providing some practical guidance. Pointing us in the right direction, it challenges us to rip away the curtain, identify the true culprit, and dismantle the dysfunctional, anti-democratic order that is capitalism.

What should replace cannibal capitalism is not so clear, however. I examine some possible scenarios in the following chapter.

6

Food for Thought: What Should Socialism Mean in the Twenty-First Century?

I began this book by noting, in chapter 1, that "capitalism" is back. How fitting, then, that I end it here by saying the same of "socialism." That word, too, has made a remarkable comeback, thanks in part to its long historical career as the preeminent name for capitalism's alternative. If the return of the c-word to public discourse reflects the current fractured state of neoliberal hegemony, we should not be surprised to see the s-word reappearing as well.

In any case, "socialism," too, is back! For decades the word was considered an embarrassment—a despised failure and relic of a bygone era. No more. At least not in the United States.[1] Today, US politicians like Bernie Sanders and Alexandria Ocasio-Cortez wear the label proudly and win support, while organizations like the Democratic Socialists of America attract new members in droves. But what exactly do they mean by "socialism"? However welcome, enthusiasm for the word does not translate automatically into serious reflection on its content. What exactly does or should "socialism" signify in the present era?

The arguments of the preceding chapters suggest an answer. The expanded conception of capitalism outlined there implies that we need an expanded conception of socialism, too. After all, once we've abandoned the view of capitalism as an economy, we can no longer understand socialism as an alternative economic system. If capital is wired to cannibalize the "non-economic" supports of commodity production, then a desirable alternative to it must do more than socialize ownership of the means of production. Over and above that desideratum—which I wholeheartedly endorse—it must also transform production's relation to its background conditions of possibility: namely, social reproduction, public power, nonhuman nature, and forms of wealth that lie outside capital's official circuits but within its reach. In other words, as I shall explain, a socialism for our time must overcome not only capital's exploitation of wage labor, but also its free riding on unwaged carework, public powers, and wealth expropriated from racialized subjects and nonhuman nature.

This point invites a disclaimer at the outset: to expand the idea of socialism is not to add epicycles to it. Far from simply appending more features to received understandings, it will be necessary to transform the very concept. That is in effect what I sought to do for capitalism in the previous chapters —by treating as structurally integral to it matters that are usually considered secondary—above all, gender/sexuality, race/empire, ecology, and democracy. Now, in the present chapter, I seek to do the same for socialism. I aim to reconceive it, too, as an institutionalized societal order, one that is as comprehensive as capitalism—and hence, can claim to be a credible alternative to it. In this way, I hope to cast new light as well on many classical topoi of socialist thought: on domination and emancipation; on class and crisis; on property, markets, and planning; and on necessary labor, free time, and social surplus. Each of those matters should assume a different guise once we view socialism, too, as more than an economy. What should appear as well are the outlines of a socialism that differs sharply from Soviet-style Communism, on the one hand, and from social democracy, on the other—a socialism for the twenty-first century.

I must begin, however, by revisiting capitalism, which is the necessary starting point for discussions of socialism. Socialism, after all, should not be a "mere ought" or utopian dream. If it is worth discussing now, it is rather because it encapsulates real, historically emergent possibilities: potentials for human freedom, well-being, and happiness that capitalism has brought within reach but cannot actualize. Equally important, socialism is a response to capitalism's impasses and injustices: to logjams that the system precipitates periodically and cannot overcome definitively; and to forms of domination that are so deeply grounded in it that they cannot be eradicated within it. Socialism, in other words, claims to remedy capitalism's ills. And so, it is there that we must begin.

What, then, exactly is capitalism? And what is wrong with it?

What is Capitalism? A Recap

We can deal with the first question briefly, by recapping the argument of the preceding chapters. There we reconceived capitalism as an institutionalized societal order that includes four non-economic conditions for the possibility of a capitalist economy. The first, elaborated in chapter 2, is a large fund of wealth expropriated from subjugated peoples, especially from racialized peoples, consisting above all in land, natural resources, and dependent unwaged or under-waged labor. Effectively stolen, this wealth serves as an ongoing stream of free or cheap productive inputs for which capital pays little or nothing. These it mixes with other inputs, including (doubly) free wage labor, whose reproduction costs it (supposedly) remunerates. The true secret of accumulation, then, is the combining of these two "exes." Absent the expropriation of subject peoples, the exploitation of free workers would not be profitable. Yet capital disavows its reliance on expropriated wealth and refuses to pay for its replenishment.

A second non-economic precondition for a capitalist economy was expounded in chapter 3: namely, a sizeable fund of unwaged and underwaged labor devoted to social reproduction, labor that is mostly performed by women. This carework, which "makes" human beings, is indispensable to what the system calls production, which makes things in order to make profits. Without reproductive work, we saw, there could be no "workers" or "labor power," no necessary or surplus labor time, no exploitation or surplus value, no profit, or accumulation of capital. Yet capital accords carework little if any value, is unconcerned to replenish it, and seeks to avoid paying for it insofar as it can.

A third non-economic precondition for a capitalist economy, discussed in chapter 4, is a large fund of free or very cheap inputs from nonhuman nature. These supply the indispensable material substratum of capitalist production: the raw materials that labor transforms; the energy that powers machines; the foodstuffs that power bodies; and a host of general environmental prerequisites such as arable land, breathable air, potable water, and the carbon-carrying capacities of the earth's atmosphere. Absent these inputs and prerequisites, there could be no economic producers or social reproducers, no wealth to expropriate or free labor to exploit, no capital or capitalist class. Yet capital treats nature as a trove of treasure to which it can help itself freely *ad infinitum* and which it need not replenish or repair.

A fourth and final precondition for a capitalist economy is a large body of public goods supplied by states and other public powers. As we saw in chapter 5, these include legal orders, repressive forces, infrastructures, money supplies, and mechanisms for managing systemic crises. Absent these public goods, and the public powers that assure them, there could be no social order, no trust, no property, no exchange—ergo, no sustained accumulation. Yet capital tends to resent public power and seeks to evade the taxes that are necessary to sustain it.

Each of these four conditions represents an indispensable pillar of a capitalist economy. Each harbors social relations, social activities, and social wealth that together form the sine qua non for accumulation. Behind capitalism's official institutions —wage labor, production, exchange, and finance—stand their necessary supports and enabling conditions: families, communities, nature; territorial states, political organizations, and civil societies; and, not least, massive amounts and multiple forms of unwaged and expropriated labor. Fundamentally integral to capitalist society, they too are constitutive elements of it.

By identifying these disavowed background conditions, we arrived at an unorthodox answer to our initial question, what is capitalism? Capitalism is not an economy, but a type of *society*—one in which an arena of economized activities and relations is marked out and set apart from other, non-economized zones, on which the former depend, but which they disavow. A capitalist society comprises an "economy" that is distinct from (and dependent on) a "polity" or political order; an arena of "economic production" that is distinct from (and dependent on) a zone of "social reproduction"; a set of exploitative relations that are distinct from (and dependent on) disavowed relations of expropriation; and a sociohistorical realm of human activity that is distinct from (and dependent on) a material substratum of nonhuman nature.

In adopting this perspective, we traded the received, narrow view of capitalism for a new, expanded view. That switch has major consequences for the project of reimagining socialism. It changes—indeed expands—our sense of what is wrong with capitalism and of what must be done to transform it.

What is Wrong with Capitalism?

Critics who assume the narrow view of capitalism see three main wrongs built into it: injustice, irrationality, and unfreedom. First, they identify the system's core injustice as the exploitation by capital of the class of free propertyless workers. The latter work many hours for free, producing enormous wealth in which they have no share. The benefits flow rather to the capitalist class, which appropriates their surplus labor and the surplus value generated by it, reinvesting the latter for its own systemically dictated purpose—namely, to accumulate ever more of it. The larger consequence is the relentless exponential growth of capital as a hostile power that dominates the very workers who produce it. This is the core injustice identified by the narrow view: the class exploitation of waged labor at the point of production. Its locus is the capitalist economy, specifically the sphere of economic production.

Second, in the narrow view, capitalism's chief irrationality is its built-in tendency to economic crisis. An economic system oriented to the limitless accumulation of surplus value, appropriated privately by for-profit firms, is inherently self-destabilizing. The drive to expand capital by increasing productivity through technical advances results in periodic drops in the rate of profit, the overproduction of goods, and the overaccumulation of capital. Attempted fixes like financialization only postpone the day of reckoning, while ensuring it will be all the more severe when it does arrive. In general, the course of capitalist development is punctuated by periodic economic crises: by boom-bust cycles, stock market crashes, financial panics, bankruptcy chains, mass liquidations of value, and mass unemployment.

Finally, the narrow view proposes that capitalism is deeply and constitutively undemocratic. Granted, it often promises democracy in the political realm. However, that promise is systematically undercut by social inequality, on the one hand, and by class power, on the other. Then, too, the capitalist workplace is exempt from any pretense of democratic self-governance. It is a sphere where capital commands and workers obey.

In general, then, the narrow view ascribes three chief wrongs to capitalism—injustice in the sense of class exploitation;

irrationality in the sense of propensity to economic crisis; and unfreedom in the sense that democracy is undercut by social inequality and class power. The trouble arises, in every case, from the internal dynamics of capitalism's *economy*. Thus, the wrongs of capitalism reside, on the narrow view, in its economic organization.

This picture is not so much wrong as incomplete. While correctly identifying the system's inherent economic ills, it fails to register a range of *non-economic* injustices, irrationalities, and unfreedoms, which are equally constitutive of it. When we adopt the expanded, "cannibal" conception, by contrast, these additional wrongs come clearly into view.

First, the cannibal view of capitalism unveils an expanded catalogue of injustices. Far from residing exclusively *within* the system's economy, these are grounded in the relations *between* the capitalist economy and its non-economic conditions of possibility. A case in point is the division between economic production—where necessary labor time is remunerated in cash wages—and social reproduction—where it is unpaid or underpaid, naturalized or sentimentalized, and recompensed in part by love. Historically gendered, this division entrenches major forms of domination at the heart of capitalist societies: women's subordination, gender binarism, and heteronormativity.

Similarly, capitalist societies institute a structural division between (doubly) free workers, who can exchange their labor power for the costs of their reproduction, and dependent "others," whose persons, lands, and labor can simply be seized. This division coincides with the global line. Hiving off the "merely" exploitable from the downright expropriable, it racializes the latter group as inherently violable. The result is to entrench a range of structural injustices, including racial oppression, imperialism (old and new), indigenous dispossession, and genocide.

Finally, capitalist societies institute a sharp division between human beings and nonhuman nature, which cease to belong to the same ontological universe. Reduced to a tap and a sink, nonhuman nature is opened to brute extractivism and instrumentalization. If this is not an injustice against "nature" (or against nonhuman animals), it is at the very least an injustice against existing and future generations of human beings who are left with an increasingly uninhabitable planet.

In general, then, an expanded view of capitalist society makes visible an expanded catalogue of structural injustices, which includes but far exceeds class exploitation. A socialist alternative must remedy these other injustices, too. Far from "merely" transforming the organization of economic production, it must also transform the latter's relation to social reproduction, and with it, the gender and sexual orders. Equally, it must end capital's free riding on nature and its expropriation of the wealth of subjugated peoples and with that, racial/imperial oppression. In sum, if socialism is to remedy capitalism's injustices, it must change not "just" the capitalist economy, but the entire institutionalized order that is capitalist society.

But that is not all. The expanded conception also enlarges our view of what counts as capitalist crisis. We can now see some built-in self-destabilizing propensities, above and beyond those internal to capitalism's economy. There is, first, a systemic tendency to cannibalize social reproduction—hence to provoke crises of care. Insofar as capital tries to avoid paying for the unwaged carework on which it depends, it periodically puts enormous pressure on the chief providers of that work: families, communities, and, above all, women. The current, financialized form of capitalist society is generating just such a crisis today, as it demands both retrenchment of public provision of social services and also increased hours of waged work per household, including from women.

The expanded view also makes visible an inherent tendency to ecological crisis. Because capital avoids paying anything close to the true replacement costs of the inputs it takes from nonhuman nature, it depletes the soil, befouls the seas, floods carbon sinks, and overwhelms the carbon-carrying capacity of the planet. Helping itself to natural wealth while disavowing the latter's repair and replacement costs, it periodically destabilizes the metabolic interaction between the human and nonhuman components of nature. We are smack up against the consequences today. What threatens to incinerate the planet is not, after all, "Humanity" but rather capitalism.

Capitalism's tendencies to ecological and social-reproductive crisis are inseparable from its constitutive need for expropriated wealth from racialized peoples: its reliance on stolen lands, coerced labor, and looted minerals; its dependence on racialized zones as dumping grounds for toxic waste and on racialized peoples as suppliers of underpaid carework, increasingly organized in global care chains. The result is an entwining of economic, ecological, and social crisis with imperialism and racial-ethnic antagonism. Neoliberalism has upped the ante here as well.

Finally, the enlarged view of capitalism discloses a structural tendency to political crisis. Here, too, capital aims to have it both ways, living off public goods for which it tries not to pay. Primed to evade taxes and to weaken state regulations, it tends to hollow out the very public powers on which it depends. The current, financialized form of capitalism takes this game to a whole new level. Megacorporations outgun territorially tethered public powers, while global finance disciplines states, making a mockery of elections that go against it and preventing anti- capitalist governments from addressing popular claims. The result is a major crisis of governance, now paired with a crisis of hegemony, as masses of people across the globe defect from established political parties and neoliberal common sense.

In general, then, the expanded view shows us that capitalism harbors multiple crisis tendencies above and beyond the economic. As explained in chapter 5, I follow Karl Polanyi (and James O'Connor) in understanding the former as "inter-realm" contradictions, lodged at the joints that separate, and connect, the capitalist economy to its non-economic background conditions of possibility. Bound to the four-D logic I explained in the previous chapters, capital has a built-in tendency to erode, destroy, or deplete—but in any case, to destabilize—its own presuppositions. Like the ouroboros, it eats its own tail. Self-cannibalization, too, forms part of what is wrong with capitalist society—and of what socialism must overcome.

There is, finally, capitalism's built-in democratic deficit. This third wrong, too, appears far larger when we adopt the expanded view of this social system. The problem is not only that bosses command on the factory floor. Nor is it only that economic inequality and class power mock every pretense to equal democratic voice in the political realm. It is equally if not more consequential that that realm had been severely truncated from the get-go. In fact, the economy/polity division radically downsizes the scope of democratic-decision-making in advance. When production is devolved to private firms, it is not we but the class of capitalists who control our relation to nature and the fate of the planet, as we saw in chapter 4. Likewise, it is not we but they who determine the shape of our working and non-working lives, deciding how we allocate our energies and time, how we interpret and satisfy our needs. By licensing private appropriation of society's surplus, finally, the system's economy/political nexus authorizes capitalists to shape the course of societal development and thereby to determine our future. All of these matters are pre-emptively removed from the political agenda in capitalist societies. Investors bent on maximal accumulation decide them behind our backs. Far from cannibalizing itself alone, then, capitalism also cannibalizes us—devouring our collective freedom to decide together how we shall live. To overcome this form of cannibalization, socialism must expand the scope of democratic political self-rule far beyond its current miserable limits.

What Is Socialism?

If socialism aims to remedy *all* capitalism's wrongs, it faces a very big job. It must invent a new societal order that overcomes not "only" class domination but also asymmetries of gender and sex, racial/ethnic/imperial oppression, and political domination across the board. Likewise, it must deinstitutionalize multiple crisis tendencies: not "just" economic and financial but also ecological, social-reproductive, and political. Finally, a socialism for the twenty-first century must vastly enlarge the purview of democracy—and not "just" by democratizing decision-making within a predefined "political" zone. More fundamentally, it must democratize the very definition and demarcation, the very frames, that constitute "the political."

Defined this way, the task of rethinking socialism for the twenty-first century is very big. If the job gets done (which is a big "if"), it will be through the combined efforts of many people, including activists and theorists, as insights gained through social struggle synergize with programmatic thinking and political organization. In hopes of contributing to this process, I want to offer three sets of brief reflections, aimed at showing how the preceding discussion casts new light on some classical topoi of socialist thought.

The first concerns institutional boundaries. These arise, as we have seen, from capitalism's institutional separations: its disjoining of production from reproduction, of exploitation from expropriation, of the economic from the political, of human society from non-human nature. As explained in the preceding chapters, these divisions are primed to become sites of crisis and stakes of struggle in capitalist societies. For socialists, therefore, the question of whether and how societal spheres are delimited from, and connected to, one another is at least as important as the question of how they are internally organized. Instead of focusing one-sidedly on the intramural organization of the economy (or for that matter, of nature, the family, or the state), socialists need to think about the economy's relation to its background conditions of possibility: to social reproduction, nonhuman nature, noncapitalized forms of wealth, and public power. If socialism is to overcome *all* institutionalized forms of capitalist irrationality, injustice, and unfreedom, it must reimagine the relations between production and reproduction, society and nature, the economic and the political.

The point is not that socialists should aim to liquidate these divisions once and for all. On the contrary, the disastrous Soviet effort to abolish the distinction between "the political" and "the economic" can stand as a general warning against liquidation. But we can—and must—re-envision the institutional boundaries that we inherit from capitalist society. We should aim, at the very least, to redraw them so that pressing matters that capitalism has relegated to the economic become political or social. We should also contemplate changing their character, making boundaries softer and more porous. We should certainly figure out how to render the various domains they separate mutually compatible and mutually responsive, non-antithetical and non-antagonistic. Surely, a socialist society must overcome capitalism's tendency to institute zero-sum games, which take away from nature, public power, and social reproduction what they give to production.

Even more important, we must reverse current priorities among those domains. Whereas capitalist societies subordinate the imperatives of social, political, and ecological reproduction to those of commodity production, itself geared to accumulation, socialists need to turn things right side up—to install the nurturing of people, the safeguarding of nature, and democratic self-rule as society's highest priorities, which trump efficiency and growth. In effect, socialism must put squarely in the foreground those matters that capital relegates to its disavowed background.

Finally, a socialism for the twenty-first century must democratize the process of institutional design. This means making the design and scope of societal domains a *political* question. In short, what capitalism has decided *for us* behind our backs should now be decided *by us* via collective democratic decision-making. Thus, we ourselves should engage in what legal theorists call "redomaining": redrawing the boundaries that demarcate societal arenas and deciding what to include within them.[2] That process can be viewed as "metapolitical"—that is, as mobilizing (second-order) political processes of redomaining to constitute (first-order) political spaces democratically.[3] Here, in effect, we ourselves decide politically which matters will be addressed politically and in which political arenas.

If it is to be genuinely democratic, however, socialist redomaining must be just. Some of what that means is already clear. First, the decision-making must be appropriately inclusive; for every matter under consideration, all those affected or subjected must be entitled to participate.[4] In addition, participation must be on equal terms; democracy requires parity of participation and so, is incompatible with structural domination.[5]

But there is another, less familiar idea that should also guide the process. Call it "pay as you go." Eschewing all forms of free riding and so-called primitive accumulation, twenty-first century socialism must ensure the sustainability of all those conditions of production that capitalism has so callously trashed. In other words: a socialist society must undertake to replenish, repair, or replace all the wealth it uses up in production and reproduction. First, it must replenish work that produces use values (including the carework that sustains people), as well as work that produces commodities. In addition, it must replace all the wealth it takes from "the outside"—from peripheral peoples and societies as well as from nonhuman nature. Finally, it must replenish the political capacities and public goods on which it draws in the course of meeting other needs. In other words: there must be no free riding of the sort that capitalism simultaneously incentivizes and disavows. This proviso is a sine qua non for overcoming the intergenerational injustice endemic to capitalist society. Only by observing it can a socialism for the twenty-first century dismantle capitalism's multiple crisis tendencies and irrationalities.

This brings me to a second set of reflections, concerning the classical socialist question of surplus. Surplus is the fund of wealth, if any, that society collectively generates in excess of what it requires to reproduce itself at its current level and in its current form. In capitalist societies, as I have already noted, surplus is treated as the private property of the capitalist class and disposed of by its owners, whom the system compels to reinvest it in hopes of producing yet more of it, on and on, without limit. This, as we saw before, is both unjust and self-destabilizing.

A socialist society must democratize control over social surplus. It must allocate surplus democratically, deciding via collective decision-making exactly what to do with existing excess capacities and resources—as well as how much excess capacity it wants to produce in the future, and indeed whether, faced with global heating, it wants to produce any surplus at all. Socialism, then, must deinstitutionalize the growth imperative hardwired into capitalist society. This does not mean, as some ecologists now argue, that we must institutionalize degrowth as a hardwired counter-imperative. It means, rather, that we must make the question of growth (how much, if any; what kind, how, and where) a political question, to be decided via multi-dimensional reflection informed by climate science. In fact, a socialism for the twenty-first century must treat all such questions as political questions, subject to democratic resolution.

Surplus can also be thought of as time: time left over after the necessary work of meeting our needs and replenishing what we've used up; hence, time that could be free time. The prospect of free time has been a central pivot of all the classical accounts of socialist freedom, including that of Marx. In the early stages of socialism, however, it's unlikely that free time would loom very large. The reason lies in the enormous unpaid bill that socialist society would inherit from capitalism. Although capitalism prides itself on its productivity, and although Marx himself considered it a veritable engine for producing surplus, I have my doubts. The trouble is, Marx reckoned surplus pretty much exclusively in the uncompensated labor time that capital takes from waged workers after they produce sufficient value to cover their own costs of living. He paid much less attention, by contrast, to the various free gifts and cheaps that capital expropriates and appropriates, and still less to its failure to cover *their* reproduction costs. What if we included *those* costs in our reckoning? What if capital had had to pay for free reproductive work, for ecological repair and replenishment, for wealth expropriated from racialized people, for public goods? How much surplus would it have really produced? That is, of course, a rhetorical question. It is unclear how exactly one would go about trying to answer it. But it *is* clear that a socialist society would inherit a hefty bill for centuries of unpaid costs.

It would also inherit a hefty bill for massive unmet human needs across the globe: needs for health care, housing, nutritious (and delicious) food, education, transportation, and so on. These too should not be counted as surplus investment, but rather as matters of absolute necessity. The same holds for the pressing and enormous job of decarbonizing the world economy—a task that is in no way optional. In general, the question of what is necessary and what is surplus assumes a different guise in light of our expanded conceptions of capitalism and of socialism.

The same is true for a third major topos of social theorizing: the role of markets in a socialist society. On this issue, the implications of the cannibal capitalism conception can be condensed in a simple formula: no markets at the top, no markets at the bottom, but possibly some markets in the in-between. Let me explain.

What I mean by "the top" is the allocation of social surplus. Assuming there is a social surplus to be allocated, it must be considered the collective wealth of the society as a whole. No private person, firm, or state can own it or have the right to dispose of it unilaterally. Truly collective property, surplus must be allocated via collective processes of decision making and planning—planning that can and must be organized democratically. Market mechanisms should play no role at this level. The rule here is neither markets nor private property at the top.

The same holds for "the bottom," by which I mean the level of basic needs: shelter, clothing, food, education, health care, transportation, communication, energy, leisure, clean water, and breathable air. It is true, of course, that we cannot specify once and for all exactly what counts as a basic need and exactly what is required to satisfy it. That too must be a subject for democratic discussion, contestation, and decision making. But whatever is decided must be provided as a matter of right, and not on the basis of ability to pay. This means that the use values we produce to meet these needs cannot be commodities. They must instead be public goods. And that points, incidentally, to a key drawback to proposals for a universal (or unconditional) basic income (UBI), which involves paying people cash to buy stuff to meet their basic needs, thereby treating basic need satisfactions as commodities. A socialist society should treat them rather as public goods. It should have no markets at the bottom.

So, no markets at the bottom or the top. But what about the in-between? Socialists should imagine the in-between as a space for experimentation with a mix of different possibilities: a space where markets could find a place, along with cooperatives, commons, self-organized associations, and self-managed projects. Many traditional socialist objections to markets would dissolve or diminish in the context I am envisioning here, as their operation would neither feed into nor be distorted by the dynamics of capital accumulation and private appropriation of social surplus. Once the top and the bottom are socialized and decommodified, the function and role of markets in the middle would be transformed. That proposition seems clear enough, even if we cannot specify now exactly how.

Many such uncertainties cry out for reflection and clarification by those who seek to develop an expanded conception of socialism for the twenty-first century. The view that I have sketched here is plainly partial and preliminary. It addresses only a subset of the most pressing and relevant questions and does so in a fashion that is frankly exploratory. Nevertheless, I hope to have demonstrated the merits of this way of approaching the question of what socialism should mean today. One such merit is the prospect of overcoming the economism of received conceptions. Another is the chance to demonstrate socialism's relevance to a broad range of current concerns beyond those centered by traditional labor movements: namely, social reproduction, structural racism, imperialism, de-democratization, and global warming. Yet a third advantage is the capacity to shed new light on some classical topoi of socialist thought, including institutional boundaries, social surplus, and the role of markets.

Beyond all that, I hope to have shown something simpler but more important: that the socialist project is well worth pursuing in the twenty-first century; that far from remaining a mere buzzword or relic of history, "socialism" must become the name for a genuine alternative to the system that is currently destroying the planet and thwarting our chances for living freely, democratically, and well.

Epilogue

Macrophage: Why COVID Is a Cannibal Capitalist Orgy

Macrophage, n.
now used primarily in immunology; literally "big eater," from the Greek μακρός (*makrós*, "large") and φαγεῖν (*phagein*, "to eat")

Most of this book was written prior to the outbreak of COVID-19. During those pre-pandemic years, as I was developing the expanded conception of capitalism, I focused on elaborating the various "hidden abodes" that enable capital accumulation in the official economy. The result, which you have before you, includes a group of chapters, each centered on one of those necessary but disavowed preconditions: racialized expropriation and social reproduction, the earth's ecology and political power. In each case, I sought to disclose the contradictory, crisis-prone character of a societal order that is structurally primed to cannibalize the very bases of its own existence: to guzzle carework and scarf up nature, to eviscerate public power and devour the wealth of racialized populations. In each case, too, I indicated that none of those feeding frenzies proceeds monologically, in isolation from the others. To the contrary, all are intertwined in the all-consuming crisis we inhabit today.

The COVID-19 outbreak offers a textbook demonstration of these entanglements. As I write now, in April 2022, the pandemic is the point where all of cannibal capitalism's contradictions converge: where cannibalization of nature and carework, of political capacity and peripheralized populations, merge in a lethal binge. A veritable orgy of capitalist dysfunction, COVID-19 establishes beyond all doubt the need to abolish this social system once and for all.

To see why, consider nature. It was none other than capital's cannibalization of that vital support of its own existence (and ours!) that exposed humans to SARS-CoV-2. Long harbored by bats in remote caves, the coronavirus that causes COVID-19 made the zoonotic leap to us in 2019 by way of some yet unidentified bridging species, possibly pangolins. But what brought the bats into contact with that intermediary, and the latter into contact with us, is already clear: namely, the combined effects of global warming, on the one hand, and tropical deforestation, on the other. What is also clear is that both of those processes are progeny of capital, driven by its insatiable hunger for profit. Together, they eviscerated the habitats of innumerable species, triggering mass migrations, creating new proximities among previously distanced but now distressed organisms, and promoting novel transfers of pathogens among them. That dynamic has already precipitated a string of viral epidemics, each passed from bats to humans via an "amplifying host": HIV via chimpanzees, Nipah via pigs, SARS via civets, MERS via camels, and now COVID-19, possibly passed via pangolins. More will come. Such epidemics are the non-accidental by-products of a societal order that puts nature at the mercy of capital. Incentivized to appropriate biophysical wealth as quickly and cheaply as possible, with no responsibility for repair or replenishment, those dedicated to amassing profit decimate rainforests and bombard the atmosphere with greenhouse gases. Hell bent on accumulation in every era, but massively empowered by neoliberalization, they have let loose an escalating cascade of lethal plagues.

COVID's effects on humans would be horrific under any conditions. But they have been incalculably worsened by another strand of the present crisis, rooted in another structural contradiction of capitalist society, also sharpened to a fever pitch in the neoliberal era. It is, after all, not "just" nature that capital has cannibalized in this period, but also public power. That too is an essential ingredient of its diet—avidly consumed in every phase of the system's development but devoured with special ferocity in the last forty years. And there's the rub. The political capacities on which financialized capital has gorged are precisely those we could have used to mitigate the pandemic. But no such luck. Well before the COVID outbreak, most states bowed to demands of "the markets" by slashing social spending, including in public health infrastructure and basic research. With some exceptions, notably Cuba, they drew down stockpiles of life-saving equipment (personal protective equipment, ventilators, syringes, medicines, and test kits), gutted diagnostic capabilities (testing, tracing, modeling, and genetic sequencing), and shrank coordination and treatment capacities (public hospitals, intensive care units, and facilities for vaccine production, storage, and distribution). Having eviscerated public infrastructure, moreover, our rulers devolved vital health care functions to profit-driven providers and insurers, pharmaceuticals and manufacturers. These firms, constitutionally uninterested in and unconstrained by the public interest, now control the lion's share of the world's health-related labor forces and raw materials, machinery and production facilities, supply chains and intellectual property, research institutions and personnel, which together determine our fates, individual and collective. Committed to the preservation of their profit streams, they form a private force majeure that blocks concerted public action on behalf of humanity. The effects are tragic but unsurprising. A social system that subjects matters of life and death to "the law of value" was structurally primed from the get-go to abandon untold millions to COVID-19.

But that is not all. The collapse of already-weak public systems converged with another structural contradiction of capitalist society, centered on social reproduction. Always a staple of capital's consumption, carework has been voraciously gobbled up by it in recent years. The same regime that divested from public-care infrastructure also broke unions and drove down wages, compelling increased hours of paid work per household, including from primary caregivers. Off-loading carework onto families and communities while siphoning off the energies needed to perform it, neoliberalism turned capitalism's inherent tendency to destabilize social reproduction into an acute care crunch. COVID's advent has intensified this strand of crisis too, dumping major new care chores on families and communities—especially onto women, who still do the lion's share of unpaid carework. Under lockdown, childcare and schooling shifted into people's homes, leaving parents to take on that burden, on top of others, in confined domestic spaces not suited to these purposes. Many employed women ended up quitting their jobs to care for kids and other relatives, while many others were laid off by employers. Both groups face major losses in position and pay if and when they rejoin the workforce. A third group, privileged to keep their jobs and work remotely from home while also performing carework, including for housebound kids, has taken multitasking to new heights of craziness. A fourth group, not strictly delimited by gender, bears the honorific "essential workers," but has been paid a pittance and treated as disposable, required to brave the threat of infection daily, along with the fear of bringing it home, in order to produce and distribute the stuff that has enabled others to shelter in place. In each of these cases, the work of social reproduction, now swollen by the pandemic, has still fallen largely to women, as it has in every phase of capitalism's history. But which women end up in which category depends on class and color.

Structural racism, after all, has been central to every phase of the system's development, not excepting the present one. Contra left-wing orthodoxies, capital accumulation proceeds not only by exploiting (doubly) free waged laborers, but also by expropriating dependent populations who've been stripped of political power and actionable rights. That distinction, between exploitation and expropriation, corresponds to the global color line. A built-in feature of capitalist society, racial-imperial predation infuses every aspect of the current crisis. At the global level, it colors the geography of ecological devastation, as capital quenches its thirst for "cheap nature" largely by seizing land, energy, and mineral wealth from racialized populations. Deprived of the means of self-defense and subject to conquest, enslavement, genocide, and dispossession, those populations bear an undue share of the global environmental load. Disproportionately vulnerable to toxic dumping, "natural disasters," and multiple lethal impacts of global warming, they now find themselves last in line for vaccination and therapeutics.

At the national level, meanwhile, color inflects the political and social-reproductive strands of the crisis, as racialized populations in many countries have been denied access to conditions that promote health: affordable, high-quality medical care, clean water, nutritious food, safe working and living conditions. No wonder, then, that their members have been disproportionately infected and killed by COVID. Hardly mysterious, the reasons are poverty and inferior health care; preexisting medical conditions linked to stress, poor nutrition, and exposure to toxins; overrepresentation in frontline jobs that cannot be performed remotely; lack of resources that would permit them to refuse unsafe work; inferior housing and living arrangements that don't allow for social distancing and facilitate transmission; and diminished access to treatment and vaccines. Together, these conditions have expanded the meaning of the slogan "Black Lives Matter," synergizing with its original reference to police violence and helping to fuel the massive protests of May and June 2020, following the murder of George Floyd at the hands of Minneapolis police.

Color, moreover, is deeply entangled with class—in the capitalist world system generally and in the present period particularly. In fact, the two are inseparable, as the category "essential worker" shows. If we leave aside medical professionals, that designation covers migrant farmworkers, immigrant meatpacking and slaughterhouse workers, Amazon warehouse pickers, UPS drivers, nursing home aides, hospital cleaners, supermarket stockers and cashiers, and gig-workers who deliver groceries and takeout meals. Especially dangerous in COVID times, these jobs are mostly low paid, nonunionized, and precarious, bereft of benefits and labor protections. Subject to intrusive supervision and control, they offer little autonomy or prospect for advancement and skill acquisition. They are also disproportionately filled by women and people of color. Taken together, these jobs, and those who perform them, represent the face of the working class in financialized capitalism. No longer epitomized by the figure of the white male miner, factory operative, and construction worker, that class now consists paradigmatically of careworkers, gig-workers, and low-wage service workers. Paid less than the costs of its reproduction (when paid at all), it is expropriated as well as exploited. COVID has exposed that dirty secret as well. By juxtaposing the "essential" character of that class's work to capital's systematic undervaluation of it, the pandemic testifies to another major defect of capitalist society: the inability of markets in labor power to accurately reckon the real worth of work.

In general, then, COVID is a veritable orgy of capitalist irrationality and injustice. By ratcheting up the system's inherent defects to the breaking point, it shines a piercing beam on all the hidden abodes of our society. Dragging them out from the shadows and into the daylight, the pandemic reveals capitalism's structural contradictions for all to see: capital's inherent drive to cannibalize nature, up to the very brink of planetary conflagration; to divert our capacities away from the truly essential work of social reproduction; to eviscerate public power to the point where it cannot solve the problems the system generates; to feed off the ever-decreasing wealth and health of racialized people; to not only exploit but also expropriate the working class. We could not ask for a better lesson in social theory. But now comes the hard part: putting that lesson to work in social practice. It's time to figure out how to starve the beast and put an end once and for all to cannibal capitalism.

Notes

1. Omnivore

1 Capital is often defined in the Marxist tradition as *self-expanding value*. But that formulation is misleading. In reality capital expands both by appropriating surplus labor time from exploited wage workers and also by expropriating un- and under-capitalized wealth from careworkers, racialized populations, and nature. It expands, in other words, not all by itself, but rather by cannibalizing *us*. I stress this point by putting the term *self* in square quotes.

2 Piero Sraffa, *Production of Commodities by Means of Commodities: Prelude to a Critique of Economic Theory* (Cambridge, UK: Cambridge University Press, 1960).

3 Immanuel Wallerstein, *Historical Capitalism* (London: Verso 1983), 39.

4 Karl Polanyi, *The Great Transformation* (Boston: Beacon Press, 1965); Nancy Fraser, "Can Society Be Commodities All the Way Down?," *Economy and Society* 43 (2014).

5 Karl Marx, *Capital*, Vol. 1, trans. Ben Fowkes (London: Penguin, 1976), 873–6.

6 Rosa Luxemburg, *The Accumulation of Capital* (New York: Monthly Review Press, 1968); David Harvey, *The New Imperialism* (Oxford: Oxford University Press, 2003), 137–82.

7 Karl Marx, *Capital*, Vol. III, trans. David Fernbach (New York: International Publishers, 1981), 949–50; John Bellamy Foster, "Marx's Theory of Metabolic Rift: Classical Foundations of Environmental Sociology," *American Journal of Sociology* 105, no. 2 (September 1996). For a critique of the Anthropocene concept, see chapter 4 of this volume.

8 Donna Haraway, "A Cyborg Manifesto: Science, Technology, and Socialist-Feminism in the Late Twentieth Century," *Socialist Review* 80 (1985).

9 Geoffrey Ingham, *The Nature of Money* (Cambridge: Cambridge

University Press, 2004); David Graeber, *Debt: The First 5,000 Years* (New York: Melville House, 2011).

10 Ellen Meiksins Wood, *Empire of Capital* (London and New York: Verso, 2003).

11 Giovanni Arrighi, *The Long Twentieth Century: Money, Power, and the Origins of Our Times* (London and New York: Verso, 1994).

12 Georg Lukács, *History and Class Consciousness: Studies in Marxist Dialectics* (London: Merlin Press, 1971).

13 Sara Ruddick, *Maternal Thinking: Towards a Politics of Peace* (London: Women's Press, 1990); Joan Trento, *Moral Boundaries: A Political Argument for an Ethic of Care* (New York: Routledge, 1993).

14 Nancy Fraser, "Struggle over Needs: Outline of a Socialist-Feminist Critical Theory of Late-Capitalist Political Culture," in *Unruly Practices: Power, Discourse, and Gender in Contemporary Social Theory* (Minneapolis: University of Minnesota Press, 1989).

15 See James O'Connor, "Capitalism, Nature, Socialism: A Theoretical Introduction," *Capitalism, Nature, Socialism* 1, no. 1 (1988), 1–22.

2. Glutton for Punishment

1 The expression "Black Marxism" comes from Cedric Robinson, who originated the notion of a distinctive Marxian tradition of Black liberation thought. See Robinson, *Black Marxism* (Chapel Hill: University of North Carolina Press, 1999). But rather than endorse that tradition, Robinson positioned himself as a critic of it. Works by some of Black Marxism's leading exponents include C. L. R. James, *The Black Jacobins* (London: Penguin Books, 1938); W. E. B. Du Bois, *Black Reconstruction in America, 1860–1880* (1938); Eric Williams, *Capitalism and Slavery* (Chapel Hill: University of North Carolina Press, 1944); Oliver Cromwell Cox, *Caste, Class, and Race: A Study of Social Dynamics* (Monthly Review Press, 1948); Stuart Hall, "Race, Articulation, and Societies Structured in Dominance," *Sociological Theories: Race and Colonialism* (UNESCO, 1980), 305–45; Walter Rodney, *How Europe Underdeveloped Africa* (Washington, DC: Howard University Press, 1981); Angela Davis, *Women, Race, and Class* (London: Women's Press, 1982); Manning Marable, *How Capitalism Underdeveloped Black America* (Brooklyn: South End Press, 1983); Barbara Fields, "Slavery, Race, and Ideology in the United States of America," *New Left Review* 181 (May–June 1990), 95–118;

Robin D. G. Kelley, *Hammer and Hoe: Alabama Communists during the Great Depression* (Chapel Hill: University of North Carolina Press, 1990) and *Race Rebels: Culture, Politics, and the Black Working Class* (New York: Free Press, 1996); and Cornel West, "The Indispensability Yet Insufficiency of Marxist Theory" and "Race and Social Theory," both in *The Cornel West Reader* (New York: Basic Civitas Books, 1999), 213–30 and 251–67.

2 This expression originally designated scholarship aimed at illuminating the relationship between law and race. It has since been hijacked by rightwing actors in the United States who use it to designate and delegitimate systematic anti-racist inquiry of any sort. I use the phrase here, and throughout this book, not pejoratively but appreciatively, to designate the broad spectrum of anti-racist and anti-imperialist theorizing that includes, but is not limited to, Black liberation theory.

3 Michael C. Dawson, *Blacks In and Out of the Left* (Cambridge, MA: Harvard University Press, 2013); Ruth Wilson Gilmore, *Golden Gulag: Prisons, Surplus, Crisis, and Opposition in Globalizing California* (Berkeley and Los Angeles: University of California Press, 2017); Cedric Johnson, *Revolutionaries to Race Leaders: Black Power and the Making of African American Politics* (Minneapolis: University of Minnesota Press, 2007); Barbara Ransby, *Making All Black Lives Matter: Reimagining Freedom in the Twenty-First Century* (Berkeley and Los Angeles: University of California Press, 2018); Keeanga-Yamahtta Taylor, *From #Black Lives Matter to Black Liberation* (Chicago: Haymarket, 2016); and Keeanga-Yamhatta Taylor, *Race for Profit: How Banks and the Real Estate Industry Undermined Black Homeownership* (University of North Carolina Press, 2021).

4 It would be false to say that Marx did not consider these processes at all. On the contrary, he wrote in *Capital*, for example, about slavery, colonialism, the expulsion of the Irish, and the "reserve army of labor." But with the exception of the last, these discussions were not systematically elaborated. Nor did they generate categories that play an integral, structural role in his conception of capitalism. See Karl Marx, *Capital*, Vol. I, trans. Ben Fowkes (London: Penguin, 1976), 781–802; 854–70; 914–26; and 931–40. By contrast, a long line of subsequent thinkers has sought to incorporate the analysis of racial oppression into Marxism. See notes 1 and 2 above. My own effort builds upon theirs, even as it also develops a distinctive conceptual argument.

5 This formulation echoes a thought of Jason Moore, who notes capital's ongoing reliance on the expropriation of unpaid work (from nature as well as from people) as a condition for the possibility of

profitable production. He writes: "Productivity-maximizing technologies revive system-wide accumulation when they set in motion a vast appropriation of uncapitalized nature. For every Amsterdam there is a Vistula Basin. For every Manchester, a Mississippi Delta." Jason W. Moore, "The Capitalocene, Part II: Accumulation by Appropriation and the Centrality of Unpaid Work/Energy," *Journal of Peasant Studies* 45 (2018).

6 As I explain in the following section, such divide-and-rule tactics mobilize racially coded status hierarchies that distinguish citizens from subjects, nationals from aliens, free individuals from slaves, "Europeans" from "natives," "whites" from "blacks," and entitled "workers" from dependent "scroungers."

7 Marx, *Capital*, Vol. 1, 873–6.

8 For another account that extends the concept of primitive accumulation beyond initial stockpiling, see Robin Blackburn, "Extended Primitive Accumulation," in *The Making of New World Slavery: From the Baroque to the Modern, 1492–1800* (London and New York: Verso, 2010).

9 The dependence of accumulation on subjectivation is a special case of a larger phenomenon. In other respects, too, capitalism's "economic subsystem" depends for its very existence on conditions external to it, including some that can only be assured by political powers. Evidently, accumulation requires a legal framework to guarantee property rights, enforce contracts, and adjudicate disputes. Equally necessary are repressive forces, which suppress rebellions, maintain order, and manage dissent. Then, too, political initiatives aimed at managing crisis have proved indispensable at various points in capitalism's history, as has public provision of infrastructure, social welfare, and, of course, money. I discuss those indispensable political functions in chapter 5 of the present volume and in "Legitimation Crisis? On the Political Contradictions of Financialized Capitalism," *Critical Historical Studies* 2, no. 2 (2015), 1–33. I focus here, by contrast, on the equally necessary function of political subjectivation.

10 Judith Shklar, *American Citizenship: The Quest for Inclusion* (Cambridge, MA: Harvard University Press, 1998).

11 Marx, *Capital*, Vol. 1, 915.

12 Nancy Fraser and Linda Gordon, "A Genealogy of 'Dependency': Tracing a Keyword of the US Welfare State," *Signs: Journal of Women in Culture and Society* 19, no. 2 (Winter 1994), 309–36. Reprinted in Nancy Fraser, *Fortunes of Feminism: From State-Managed Capitalism to Neoliberal Crisis* (London and New York: Verso, 2013).

13 I am suggesting that the situation of racialized labor in state-

managed capitalism combined elements of expropriation with elements of exploitation. On one hand, workers of color in the US core were paid a wage, but one that was less than the average socially necessary costs of their reproduction. On the other, they had the formal status of free persons and US citizens, but they could not call on public powers to vindicate their rights; on the contrary, those who were supposed to protect them from violence were often perpetrators of it. Thus, their status amalgamated both political and economic aspects of the two exes. It is better understood in this way, as an amalgam or hybrid of exploitation and expropriation, than via the more familiar concept of "super-exploitation." Although that term is undeniably evocative, it focuses exclusively on the economics of the racial wage gap, while ignoring the status differential. My approach, in contrast, aims to disclose the entwinement of economic predation with political subjection. For a discussion of super-exploitation, see, e.g., Ruy Mauro Marini, *Dialéctica de la dependencia* (Mexico City: Ediciones Era, 1973).

14 BRICS is an acronym for these countries: Brazil, Russia, India, China, and South Africa.

15 For progressive neoliberalism, see Nancy Fraser, "The End of Progressive Neoliberalism," *Dissent* (Spring 2017). See also Nancy Fraser, *The Old Is Dying and the New Cannot Be Born: From Progressive Neoliberalism to Trump and Beyond* (London and New York: Verso, 2019).

3. Care Guzzler

1 An earlier, French-language version of this chapter was delivered in Paris on June 14, 2016, as the Marc Bloch Lecture of the École des hautes études en sciences sociales and is available on the École's website. I thank Pierre-Cyrille Hautcœur for the lecture invitation, Johanna Oksala for stimulating discussions, Mala Htun and Eli Zaretsky for helpful comments, and Selim Heper for research assistance.

2 Many feminist theorists have made versions of this argument. Iconic Marxist feminist formulations include Eli Zaretsky, *Capitalism, the Family, and Personal Life* (London: Pluto Press, 1986); and Lise Vogel, *Marxism and the Oppression of Women* (Boston: Brill, 2013). Another powerful formulation is Nancy Folbre, *The Invisible Heart* (New York: New Press, 2002). Later elaborations by social-reproduction theorists include Barbara Laslett and Johanna Brenner, "Gender and Social Reproduction," *Annual Review of*

Sociology 15 (1989); Kate Bezanson and Meg Luxton, eds., *Social Reproduction* (Montreal: McGill–Queen's University Press, 2006); Isabella Bakker, "Social Reproduction and the Constitution of a Gendered Political Economy," *New Political Economy* 12, no. 4 (2007); *Social Reproduction Theory: Remapping Class, Recentering Oppression*, ed. Tithi Bhattacharya (Pluto Books, 2017); Susan Ferguson, *Women and Work: Feminism, Labor, and Social Reproduction* (Pluto, 2019); and Cinzia Arruzza, Tithi Bhattacharya, and Nancy Fraser, *Feminism for the 99%: A Manifesto* (Verso, 2019).

3 Louise Tilly and Joan Scott, *Women, Work, and Family* (London: Routledge, 1987).

4 Karl Marx and Friedrich Engels, "Manifesto of the Communist Party," in *The Marx-Engels Reader* (New York: W.W. Norton & Co., 1978), 487–8; Friedrich Engels, *The Origin of the Family, Private Property, and the State* (Chicago: Charles H. Kerr, 1902), 90–100.

5 Nancy Woloch, *A Class by Herself* (Princeton, NJ: Princeton University Press, 2015).

6 Karl Polanyi, *The Great Transformation* (Boston: Beacon Press, 2001), 87, 138–9, 213.

7 Ava Baron, "Protective Labour Legislation and the Cult of Domesticity," *Journal of Family Issues* 2, no. 1 (1981).

8 Maria Mies, *Patriarchy and Accumulation on a World Scale* (London: Bloomsbury Academic, 2014), 74.

9 Eli Zaretsky, *Capitalism, the Family, and Personal Life* (London: Pluto Press, 1986); Stephanie Coontz, *The Social Origins of Private Life* (London: Verso, 1988).

10 Judith Walkowitz, *Prostitution and Victorian Society* (Cambridge, UK: Cambridge University Press, 1980); Barbara Hobson, *Uneasy Virtue: The Politics of Prostitution and the American Reform Tradition* (Chicago: University of Chicago Press, 1990).

11 Angela Davis, "Reflections on the Black Woman's Role in the Community of Slaves," *Massachusetts Review* 13, no. 2 (1972).

12 David Wallace Adams, *Education for Extinction: American Indians and the Boarding School Experience, 1875–1928* (Lawrence: University Press of Kansas, 1995); Ward Churchill, *Kill the Indian, Save the Man: The Genocidal Impact of American Indian Residential Schools* (San Francisco: City Lights, 2004).

13 Gayatri Spivak, "Can the Subaltern Speak?," in *Marxism and the Interpretation of Culture*, ed. Cary Nelson and Lawrence Grossberg (London: Macmillan Education, 1988), 305.

14 Nancy Fraser, "A Triple Movement? Parsing the Politics of Crisis after Polanyi," *New Left Review* 81 (May-June 2013) pp. 119–132.

15 Michel Foucault, "Governmentality," in *The Foucault Effect*, ed. Graham Burchell, Colin Gordon, and Peter Miller (Chicago: University of Chicago Press, 1991), 87–104; Foucault, *The Birth of Biopolitics: Lectures at the Collège de France, 1978–1979* (New York: Palgrave Macmillan, 2010), 64.

16 Kristin Ross, *Fast Cars, Clean Bodies: Decolonization and the Reordering of French Culture* (Cambridge, MA, 1996); Dolores Hayden, *Building Suburbia: Green Fields and Urban Growth, 1820–2000* (New York: Pantheon, 2003); Stuart Ewen, *Captains of Consciousness: Advertising and the Social Roots of the Consumer Culture* (New York: Basic Books, 2008).

17 In this era, state support for social reproduction was financed by tax revenues and dedicated funds to which both metropolitan workers and capital contributed, in different proportions, depending on the relations of class power within a given state. But those revenue streams were swollen with value siphoned from the periphery through profits from foreign direct investment and through trade based on unequal exchange. See Raúl Prebisch, *The Economic Development of Latin America and Its Principal Problems* (New York: UN Department of Economic Affairs, 1950); Paul Baran, *The Political Economy of Growth* (New York: Monthly Review Press, 1957); Geoffrey Pilling, "Imperialism, Trade, and 'Unequal Exchange': The Work of Aghiri Emmanuel," *Economy and Society* 2, no. 2 (1973); Gernot Köhler and Arno Tausch, *Global Keynesianism: Unequal Exchange and Global Exploitation* (New York: Nova Science Publishers, 2001).

18 Jill Quadagno, *The Color of Welfare: How Racism Undermined the War on Poverty* (Oxford: Oxford University Press, 1994); Ira Katznelson, *When Affirmative Action Was White: An Untold History of Racial Inequality in Twentieth-Century America* (New York: W.W. Norton & Co., 2005).

19 Jacqueline Jones, *Labor of Love, Labor of Sorrow: Black Women, Work, and the Family from Slavery to the Present* (New York: Vintage, 1985); and Evelyn Nakano Glenn, Forced to Care: Coercion and Caregiving in America (Cambridge, MA: Harvard University Press, 2010).

20 Nancy Fraser, "Women, Welfare, and the Politics of Need Interpretation," in *Unruly Practices: Power, Discourse, and Gender in Contemporary Social Theory* (Minneapolis: University of Minnesota Press, 1989); Barbara Nelson, "Women's Poverty and Women's Citizenship," *Signs: Journal of Women in Culture and Society* 10, no. 2 (1985); Diana Pearce, "Women, Work, and Welfare," in *Working Women and Families*, ed. Karen Wolk Feinstein (Beverly Hills, CA: Sage, 1979); Johanna Brenner, "Gender,

Social Reproduction, and Women's Self-Organization," *Gender and Society* 5, no. 3 (1991).

21 Hilary Land, "Who Cares for the Family?," *Journal of Social Policy* 7, no. 3 (1978); Harriet Holter, ed., *Patriarchy in a Welfare Society* (Oxford: Oxford University Press, 1984); Mary Ruggie, *The State and Working Women* (Princeton, NJ: Princeton University Press, 1984); Birte Siim, "Women and the Welfare State," in *Gender and Caring*, ed. Clare Ungerson (London and New York: Harvester Wheatsheaf, 1990); Ann Shola Orloff, "Gendering the Comparative Analysis of Welfare States," *Sociological Theory* 27, no. 3 (2009).

22 Adrienne Roberts, "Financing Social Reproduction," *New Political Economy* 18, no. 1 (2013).

23 The fruit of an unlikely alliance between free marketeers and "new social movements," the new regime is scrambling all the usual political alignments, pitting "progressive" neoliberal feminists like Hillary Clinton against authoritarian nationalist populists like Donald Trump.

24 Elizabeth Warren and Amelia Warren Tyagi, *The Two-Income Trap: Why Middle-Class Parents Are Going Broke* (New York: Basic Books, 2003).

25 Arlie Hochschild, "Love and Gold," in *Global Woman: Nannies, Maids, and Sex Workers in the New Economy*, ed. Barbara Ehrenreich and Arlie Hochschild (New York: Henry Holt & Co., 2002), 15–30.

26 Jennifer Bair, "On Difference and Capital," *Signs: Journal of Women in Culture and Society* 36, no. 1 (2010).

27 "Apple and Facebook Offer to Freeze Eggs for Female Employees," *Guardian*, October 15, 2014. Importantly, this benefit is no longer reserved exclusively for the professional-technical-managerial class. The US Army now makes egg freezing available gratis to enlisted women who sign up for extended tours of duty: "Pentagon to Offer Plan to Store Eggs and Sperm to Retain Young Troops," *New York Times*, February 3, 2016. Here the logic of militarism overrides that of privatization. To my knowledge, no one has yet broached the looming question of what to do with the eggs of a female soldier who dies in conflict.

28 Courtney Jung, *Lactivism: How Feminists and Fundamentalists, Hippies and Yuppies, and Physicians and Politicians Made Breastfeeding Big Business and Bad Policy* (New York: Basic Books, 2015), esp. 130–1. The Affordable Care Act (aka "Obamacare") now mandates that health insurers provide such pumps free to their beneficiaries. Thus, this benefit, too, is no longer the exclusive prerogative of privileged women. The effect is to create a huge new

market for manufacturers, who are producing the pumps in very large batches in the factories of their Chinese subcontractors. See Sarah Kliff, "The Breast Pump Industry Is Booming, Thanks to Obamacare," *Washington Post*, January 4, 2013.

29 Lisa Belkin, "The Opt-Out Revolution," *New York Times*, October 26, 2003; Judith Warner, *Perfect Madness: Motherhood in the Age of Anxiety* (New York: Penguin, 2006); Lisa Miller, "The Retro Wife," *New York*, March 17, 2013; Anne-Marie Slaughter, "Why Women Still Can't Have It All," *Atlantic*, July–August 2012, and *Unfinished Business* (New York: Random House, 2015); Judith Shulevitz, "How to Fix Feminism," *New York Times*, June 10, 2016.

4. Nature in the Maw

1 My account of capitalism's ecological contradiction is indebted to James O'Connor's groundbreaking theorization of "the second contradiction of capitalism." He paved the way by drawing on the thought of Karl Polanyi to conceptualize the "conditions of production" and the tendency of capital to undermine them. See "The Second Contradiction of Capitalism, with an Addendum on the Two Contradictions of Capitalism," in James O'Connor, *Natural Causes: Essays in Ecological Marxism* (New York: Guilford, 1998), 158–77. John Bellamy Foster correctly notes some reductionist aspects of O'Connor's account in "Capitalism and Ecology: The Nature of the Contradiction," *Monthly Review* 54, no. 4 (2002), 6–16. But these are not essential to O'Connor's central vision and play no role in my adaptation of his insights.

2 Jason W. Moore, *Capitalism in the Web of Life: Ecology and the Accumulation of Capital* (London and New York: Verso, 2015). Unfortunately, Moore appears to assume that Nature III can simply replace Nature I, which he proceeds to dismiss as "Cartesian." That assumption is politically disabling, as it effectively invalidates climate science. It is also conceptually confused. As I explain below, those conceptions of nature are not in fact incompatible and can be deployed in concert. For more on my differences with Moore, see Nancy Fraser and Rahel Jaeggi, *Capitalism: A Conversation in Critical Theory*, ed. Brian Milstein (Cambridge, UK: Polity Press, 2018), 94–6.

3 One should make use of all three conceptions of Nature. Each pertains to a different level of analysis and genre of inquiry: Nature I to biophysical science; Nature II to structural analysis of capitalist society; Nature III to historical materialism. Properly

understood, they do not contradict one another. The appearance of contradiction arises only when one fails to distinguish the levels and confounds the conceptions. Thus, the current debate between critical realists and social constructivists (or "anti-Cartesians") is largely misplaced. Each side fastens on one conception, which it illegitimately totalizes, while wrongfully excluding the others. Cf. Andreas Malm, *The Progress of This Storm: Nature and Society in a Warming World* (London and New York: Verso, 2018).

4 I owe the terms "developmental" and "epochal" crises to Jason Moore, who has adapted them for ecocritical theory from Immanuel Wallerstein and Giovanni Arrighi. See Moore's essay, "*The Modern World System* as Environmental History? Ecology and the Rise of Capitalism," *Theory and Society* 32, no. 3 (2003).

5 For the distinction between "somatic" and "exosomatic" energy regimes, see J. R. McNeill, *Something New Under the Sun: An Environmental History of the 20th Century* (New York: W. W. Norton & Co., 2000), esp. 10–16.

6 Jason W. Moore, "Potosí and the Political Ecology of Underdevelopment, 1545–1800," *Journal of Philosophical Economics* 4, no. 1 (2010), 58–103.

7 There are good accounts of all this in Philippe Descola's brilliant book, *Beyond Nature and Culture*, trans. Janet Lloyd (Chicago: University of Chicago Press, 2014) and in Carolyn Merchant's classic, *The Death of Nature: Women, Ecology, and the Scientific Revolution* (San Francisco: HarperOne, 1990).

8 Andreas Malm, "The Origins of Fossil Capital: From Water to Steam in the British Cotton Industry," *Historical Materialism* 21 (2013), 15–68.

9 Matthew T. Huber, "Energizing Historical Materialism: Fossil Fuels, Space and the Capitalist Mode of Production," *Geoforum* 40 (2008) 105–15.

10 The expression "metabolic rift" comes from Marx via John Bellamy Foster, as does this account of the disruption on the soil-nutrient cycle. See Foster, "Marx's Theory of Metabolic Rift: Classical Foundations for Environmental Sociology," *American Journal of* Sociology 105, no. 2 (1999), 366–405.

11 John Bellamy Foster, Brett Clark, and Richard York, *The Ecological Rift: Capitalism's War on the Earth* (New York: New York University Press, 2011).

12 This expression comes from Jason W. Moore, "The Rise of Cheap Nature," in *Anthropocene or Capitalocene? Nature, History, and the Crisis of Capitalism*, ed. Jason W. Moore (Oakland: PM Press, 2016), 78–115.

13 Alf Hornborg, "Footprints in the Cotton Fields: The Industrial

Revolution as Time-Space Appropriation and Environmental Load Displacement," *Ecological Economics* 59, no. 1 (2006), 74–81.

14 Aaron G. Jakes, *Egypt's Occupation: Colonial Economism and the Crises of Capitalism* (Redwood City, CA: Stanford University Press, 2020).

15 See, for example, Mike Davis, "The Origins of the Third World," *Antipode* 32, no. 1 (2000), 48–89; Alf Hornborg, "The Thermodynamics of Imperialism: Toward an Ecological Theory of Unequal Exchange," in *The Power of the Machine: Global Inequalities of Economy, Technology, and Environment* (Lanham, MD: AltaMira 2001), 35–48; Joan Martinez-Alier, "The Ecological Debt," *Kurswechsel* 4 (2002), 5–16; John Bellamy Foster, Brett Clark, and Richard York, "Imperialism and Ecological Metabolism," in *The Ecological Rift: Capitalism's War on the Earth* (New York: Monthly Review Press, 2011), 345–74.

16 Joan Martinez-Alier, *The Environmentalism of the Poor: A Study of Ecological Conflicts and Valuation* (Cheltenham, UK: Edward Elgar, 2003).

17 I owe this expression, which inverts Joan Martinez-Alier's "environmentalism of the poor," to Peter Dauvergne, *Environmentalism of the Rich* (Cambridge MA: The M.I.T. Press, 2016).

18 For a masterful reconstruction of nineteenth- and twentieth-century socialist environmentalism in England, see John Bellamy Foster, *The Return of Nature: Socialism and Ecology* (New York: Monthly Review Press, 2020). Among the many recent extensions of this tradition, see Murray Bookchin, *Social Ecology and Communalism* (Chico, CA: AK Press, 2005), and Michael Löwy, *Ecosocialism: A Radical Alternative to Capitalist Catastrophe* (Chicago: Haymarket, 2015).

19 Timothy Mitchell, "Carbon Democracy," *Economy and Society* 38, no. 3 (2009), 399–432.

20 Alyssa Battistoni, "Free Gifts: Nature, Households, and the Politics of Capitalism," PhD dissertation, Yale University, 2019.

21 Susanne Friedberg, *Fresh: A Perishable History* (2010).

22 Mitchell, "Carbon Democracy."

23 Karl Jacoby, *Crimes against Nature: Squatters, Poachers, Thieves, and the Hidden History of Conservation* (Berkeley: University of California Press, 2014).

24 For "misframing," see Nancy Fraser, "Reframing Justice in a Globalizing World," *New Left Review*, n.s., 36, (Nov–Dec 2005), 69–88.

25 Adrian Parr, *The Wrath of Capital: Neoliberalism and Climate Change Politics* (New York: Columbia University Press, 2013)

26 The best account of dispossession through this marriage of biotech

and intellectual property remains Vandana Shiva's "Life Inc: Biology and the Expansion of Capitalist Markets," *Sostenible?* 2 (2000), 79–92.

27 Larry Lohmann, "Financialization, Commodification, and Carbon: The Contradictions of Neoliberal Climate Policy," *Socialist Register* 48 (2012), 85–107.

28 Martin O'Connor, "On the Misadventures of Capitalist Nature," in *Is Capitalism Sustainable? Political Economy and the Politics of Ecology*, ed. Martin O'Connor (New York: Guilford Press, 1994), 125–51; Joan Martinez-Alier, *The Environmentalism of the Poor: A Study of Ecological Conflicts and Valuation* (Cheltenham, UK: Edward Elgar, 2003).

29 The point parallels one that Black- and socialist-feminists have repeatedly made about single-issue feminism, which purports to isolate "genuine" gender issues from "extraneous" concerns and thereby ends up with a "bourgeois" or corporate feminism tailored to the situation of professional-managerial women, for whom alone those concerns are extraneous.

5. Butchering Democracy

1 I have selected these expressions to represent a range of different perspectives in democratic theory, those respectively of William E. Connolly, Andreas Kalyvas, Chantal Mouffe, and Seyla Benhabib. But I could have chosen others as well.

2 Colin Crouch, *The Strange Non-death of Neoliberalism* (Cambridge, UK: Polity Press, 2011).

3 Wolfgang Streeck, *Buying Time: The Delayed Crisis of Democratic Capitalism* (London and New York: Verso, 2014).

4 Wendy Brown, *Undoing the Demos: Neoliberalism's Stealth Revolution* (New York: Zone Books, 2015).

5 Stephen Gill, "New Constitutionalism, Democratisation, and Global Political Economy," *Pacifica Review* 10, no. 1 (1998), 23–38. For a more recent statement, see Stephen Gill, "Market Civilization, New Constitutionalism, and World Order," in *New Constitutionalism and World Order*, ed. Stephen Gill and A. Claire Cutler (Cambridge, UK: Cambridge University Press, 2015), 29–44.

6 Giovanni Arrighi, *The Long Twentieth Century: Money, Power, and the Origins of Our Time* (London and New York: Verso, 1994).

7 Ellen Meiksins Wood, "The Separation of the Economic and the Political in Capitalism," *New Left Review* 127 (1981), 66–95.

8 Hannah Arendt, *The Origins of Totalitarianism* (New York:

Harcourt, Brace, & Jovanovich, 1973). For the conflict between the trans-territorial thrust of limitless accumulation and the territorial logic of political rule, see also David Harvey, "The 'New' Imperialism: Accumulation by Dispossession," *Socialist Register* 40 (2014), 63–87.

9 Karl Polanyi, *The Great Transformation*, 2nd ed. (Boston: Beacon, 2001).

10 The exception is the United States, which can simply print more of the dollars that serve as "world money."

11 Crouch, *The Strange Non-death of Neoliberalism*

12 Reinhart Koselleck, "Crisis," trans. Michaela, W. Richter, *Journal of the History of Ideas* 67, no. 2 (April 2006), 357–400.

13 For a fuller analysis of the hegemonic dimension of the present crisis of democracy, see Nancy Fraser, *The Old Is Dying and the New Cannot Be Born* (London and New York: Verso, 2019).

14 For a fuller discussion of the COVID pandemic as an "orgy of capitalist irrationality and injustice," see the Epilogue.

15 Fraser, *The Old Is Dying and the New Cannot Be Born* (London and New York: Verso, 2019).

16 Walter Benjamin, "Paralipomena to 'On the Concept of History,'" in *Walter Benjamin: Selected Writings*, Vol. 4, *1938–40*, ed. Howard Eiland and Michael W. Jennings, trans. Edmund Jephcott et al. (Cambridge, MA: Belknap Press, 2006), 402. The line is from one of the preparatory notes to "On the Concept of History" but does not appear in the final version. The full quotation reads as follows: "Marx said that revolutions are the locomotive of world history. But perhaps things are very different. It may be that revolutions are the act by which the human race travelling in the train applies the emergency brake."

6. Food for Thought

1 If the resurgence of interest in socialism is largely a US phenomenon, that is probably because the word had so little currency here in recent decades that it escaped the association with neoliberalism that tarnished it elsewhere. In Europe especially, Socialist parties played major roles in the consolidation of neoliberal policy, thereby giving the term a bad odor, above all for activist youth. In the United States, by contrast, anti-socialist sentiment comes not from leftwing opponents of neoliberalism but from rightwing forces that recycle Cold War tropes. The latter's "old-school" posture may actually enhance the term's attractiveness to young militants, even infusing it with special cachet.

2 Mariana Prandini Assis, "Boundaries, Scales and Binaries of Women's Human Rights: An Examination of Feminist Confrontations in the Transnational Legal Sphere," PhD dissertation, 2019, The New School for Social Research.

3 Nancy Fraser, *Reframing Justice: The 2004 Spinoza Lectures* (Amsterdam: Van Gorcum, 2005) and "Reframing Justice in a Globalizing World," *New Left Review* 36 (November–December 2005), pp. 69–88.

4 For a fuller discussion of this point, see Fraser, "Reframing Justice," and Nancy Fraser, "Publicity, Subjection, Critique: A Reply to My Critics," in *Transnationalizing the Public Sphere*, ed. Kate Nash (Malden, MA: Polity Press, 2014).

5 For parity of participation and the incompatibility of democracy and domination, see Nancy Fraser and Axel Honneth, *Redistribution or Recognition? A Political-Philosophical Exchange*, trans. Joel Golb, James Ingram, and Christiane Wilke (London: Verso, 2003).

Index